Meeting St. Paul Today

MEETING
St. Paul
TODAY

Daniel J. Harrington, SJ

LOYOLA PRESS.
A JESUIT MINISTRY
Chicago

LOYOLAPRESS.
A JESUIT MINISTRY

3441 N. Ashland Avenue
Chicago, Illinois 60657
(800) 621-1008
www.loyolapress.com

Map on p. 14 created by THINK Design Group LLC.

Cover image: Corbis
Cover design by Anni Betts, Kathryn Seckman Kirsch
Interior design by Kathryn Seckman Kirsch

Library of Congress Cataloging-in-Publication Data
Harrington, Daniel J.
  Meeting St. Paul today / Daniel J. Harrington.
    p. cm.
  Includes bibliographical references.
  ISBN-13: 978-0-8294-2734-9
  ISBN-10: 0-8294-2734-1
  1. Bible. N.T. Epistles of Paul—Criticism, interpretation, etc. I. Title.
II. Title: Meeting Saint Paul today.
  BS2650.52.H37 2008
  225.9'2—dc22
                                                     2008023395

Printed in the United States of America
08 09 10 11 12 13 Versa 10 9 8 7 6 5 4 3 2

Contents

A Year Dedicated to the Apostle Paul

Pope Benedict XVI has proclaimed the period from June 29, 2008 to June 29, 2009 "the Pauline Year." This is meant to commemorate the 2,000th anniversary of the apostle's birth. While biblical scholars debate the precise year of Paul's birth, the observance of the Pauline Year is surely a good opportunity to reflect on Paul as one of the most influential and important figures in the history of the Christian faith.

Pope Benedict has had a longstanding devotion to Paul, and his first official act outside the Vatican in April 2005 was to visit the apostle's tomb at the Basilica of St. Paul Outside the Walls in Rome. In that homily he stated:

> Christ's passion led him to preach the Gospel not only with the word, but also with his very life, which was ever more conformed to that of his Lord. In the end, Paul proclaimed Christ with martyrdom, and his blood, together with that of Peter and of witnesses of the Gospel, watered this land and made fruitful the Church of Rome.

Pope Benedict's hope is that the Pauline Year will rekindle interest in Paul's life and writings, not only among Catholics but also among other Christians as well as Jews.

I have long wanted to write a short book on Paul that might help introduce him and his writings to the general public. The suggestion from Joseph Durepos of Loyola Press that I write such a book in connection with the Pauline Year came at an opportune time.

In my opinion, the best way to meet Paul today is to consider what Paul wrote about himself and what Luke wrote about him in the Acts of the Apostles (chapter 1); to read carefully the letters that Paul wrote to early Christian communities (chapter 2) and the letters that admirers wrote in his name (chapter 3); to learn some basic principles for reading and interpreting a Pauline text (chapter 4); and to reflect briefly on Paul's significance for us today (chapter 5). In the first and fourth chapters I have adapted some material from my articles in *The Bible Today* and in *Church.**

I've had the privilege to study, teach, and preach on the Pauline writings for almost forty years. I love these texts and never fail to be stimulated and challenged by them. When I read them, I often recall Karl Barth's comment in the preface to the first edition (1918) of his *Epistle to the Romans*: "If we rightly understand ourselves, our problems are the problems of Paul; and if we be enlightened by the brightness of his answers, those answers must be ours." My hope is that the readers of this book may come to see the truth of Barth's statement, and that the Pauline Year of 2008–2009 may exercise its positive effects for many years to come.

The Bible Today issue 42/4 (2004) 201–206; *Church* issue 14/3 (1998) 9–14.

1

Who Was Paul the Apostle?

Next to Jesus, Paul is the most prominent figure in the New Testament. Of the twenty-seven documents that constitute the New Testament, thirteen are letters attributed to Paul. Also, more than half of the Acts of the Apostles describes Paul's conversion and subsequent activities on behalf of the spread of the good news about Jesus (the gospel).

Where We Learn about the Life of Paul

These ancient sources tell us a lot about Paul, but they do not tell us all that we would like to know. Paul was not a professor who wrote essays on theological topics. Rather, he was an apostle—one who preached the gospel and taught the Christian community. Paul wrote his letters in response to problems that had arisen mainly in the Christian communities that Paul himself had founded. These communities—churches—were extensions of his apostolic ministry. Because Paul's theology developed out of his work with the Christian community (as opposed to being formed in what today would be a seminary or graduate school setting), Paul is best classified as a *pastoral theologian*. He was a missionary and a pastor.

When dispensing pastoral advice, Paul sometimes refers to himself and his own experiences. Of course, these statements are the very best sources for information about Paul and his activities. But he never gives us anything like what we would call an autobiography. The biblical writers, like most writers in ancient times, did not talk much about themselves. They especially avoided describing their feelings and explaining the psychological processes going on within them. So there are limits to what we can learn about Paul even from his own letters.

The author of the Acts of the Apostles was Luke, apparently the same person who composed the Gospel that bears his name (Acts 1:1–2). Luke gives a great deal of attention to the apostle Paul and his missionary endeavors. Throughout Christian history, Luke has generally been regarded as one of Paul's coworkers and even as a companion of Paul in his work as an apostle. In Acts 16 especially there is a good deal of "we" language, suggesting that the author of Acts personally accompanied Paul on some of his journeys and is giving us eyewitness testimony.

However, modern scholars have recognized that Luke (even if he was Paul's coworker and companion) had certain distinctive theological ideas of his own, was a learned and sophisticated writer (Luke 1:1–4), and often shaped historical facts to strengthen his theological interpretations. Luke tells us a lot about Paul, and what he writes cannot be ignored. But there are also limits to what we can learn about Paul from Acts. For example, from Acts we would not know that Paul wrote letters to early Christian communities!

Paul's Early Life

According to Acts 22:3, Paul was "a Jew, born in Tarsus in Cilicia." Cilicia was a Roman province on the southeastern coast of Asia Minor (present-day Turkey). In Acts 21:39 Tarsus is described as "an important city." It was a major commercial and cultural center linking east and west in the Roman Empire. When exactly Paul was born is not clear. In his letter to Philemon, written in A.D. 54 or 55, he describes himself as "an old man" (v. 9). However, the Greek word used here can also be read as "ambassador." And even "old man" is quite vague. Most scholars place Paul's birth around the time of Jesus' birth, with some putting it a few years before and others a few years afterward.

According to his own testimony in Philippians 3:5, Paul was a "Hebrew born of Hebrews," a member of the tribe of Benjamin, and circumcised on the eighth day. His Hebrew name was "Saul." The name "Paul" was most likely his "Gentile" name to be used outside the Jewish community and was given to him probably at birth and not only at his conversion to become a follower of Jesus. Paul certainly had strong credentials as a Jew.

In Acts 22:25–29, Paul claims also to be a Roman citizen, which was somewhat unusual for a Jew. When the Roman official observes that it had cost him a large sum of money to get his own citizenship, Paul responds, "But I was born a citizen."

The implication may be that Paul's parents had been slaves of the occupying Romans and managed to purchase their own freedom and to obtain Roman citizenship, which they in turn handed on to Paul.

It appears that Paul spent his early years in Tarsus, where he was part of the local Jewish community. Thus he belonged to the *Diaspora* of Israel—that is, Jews dispersed outside the land of Israel. In Tarsus, Paul would have learned to speak, read, and write in the Greek language, and he would have had some exposure to Greek and Roman culture. His mastery of the Greek language and his use of various classical rhetorical devices in his letters show a fairly high level of non-Jewish education. The mixed atmosphere in which Paul was raised is often characterized as Hellenistic Judaism, because Jews were exposed to the language, customs, and educational system that were rooted in ancient Greece.

Somewhere along the line, perhaps from his parents, Paul learned the trade of tent making or leather working of some kind (Acts 18:3). Practice of this trade enabled Paul to support himself and his missionary activity (1 Thessalonians 2:9; 1 Corinthians 9:6) without having to rely on financial support from others. It also may have provided him the opportunity to meet and influence his colleagues in the marketplace. It certainly linked him with the couple named Aquila and Prisca (also known as Priscilla in Acts), who were active in the churches at Rome and Corinth (Acts 18:2–3).

The only ancient physical description of Paul comes from the late second-century work known as the *Acts of Paul and Thecla*:

"A man small of stature, with a bald head and crooked legs, in a good state of body, with eyebrows meeting and nose somewhat hooked, full of friendliness." How historically accurate this description was is debated among scholars. Paul's opponents, quoted in 2 Corinthians, claimed that his "bodily presence is weak, and his speech contemptible" (10:10). Rather than rebutting these charges directly, Paul accepts them and goes on to argue that they only prove that God's "power is made perfect in weakness" (12:9). In the same context he complains about "a thorn . . . in the flesh" (12:7). The precise nature of this problem is not specified, leading to speculations ranging from a speech impediment to epilepsy. Again Paul offers no diagnostic details and prefers to reflect on its positive theological value in keeping him "from being too elated."

Paul's Life as a Jew

Among the various movements within the Judaism of his time, Paul chose to be a Pharisee (Philippians 3:5). In the Gospels the Pharisees emerge as the chief rivals of Jesus. They were a Jewish sect that arose in the second century B.C. While dedicated to exact observance of the Mosaic Law (the Torah), they were also the progressives (at least in comparison with the Sadducees and Essenes) among the Jewish religious movements of their day. They were often trying to adapt Jewish practices to both the letter of the Law and the changing realities of everyday life. An important feature of their movement was communal meals, which served as occasions for religious sharing. In their zeal the Pharisees sought to extend the laws of ritual purity pertaining to priests in the Jerusalem temple to other Jews, thus forming a spiritual priesthood of all Jews. At some points in Jewish history, between the second century B.C. and the first century A.D., the Pharisees had great political influence, especially under Queen Alexandra (76–67 B.C.). At other times they were out of favor, and so withdrew from the political struggles and tended to more traditional religious and legal matters.

According to Acts 22:3, Paul had a first-class Jewish education. He is quoted as saying that he was "brought up in this city [Jerusalem] at the feet of Gamaliel, educated strictly according to our ancestral law, being zealous for God, just as all of you are today." According to Acts 5:34–39, a certain Pharisee named Gamaliel ("a teacher of the Law") showed admirable wisdom and restraint when he counseled other Jews that the early Christians should be allowed to prove by their actions and results whether their movement was from God or not. Exposure to this kind of education under Gamaliel would help explain Paul's great knowledge of Scripture and his ability to make an argument on the basis of various biblical texts, as he does frequently in his letters. It would also place him in Jerusalem around the time when the early Christian movement emerged.

Paul the Persecutor

Paul never claims to have met the earthly Jesus. But he often confesses that in his "earlier life in Judaism I was violently persecuting the church of God and was trying to destroy it" (Galatians

1:13; 1:23; 1 Corinthians 15:9). According to Acts 7:58 and 8:1 Paul was present at, and approved of, the killing of Stephen, the first Christian martyr, in Jerusalem. Whatever Paul's actual role in this execution was, the connection with Stephen's death may explain more precisely why and to what extent Paul became a persecutor of the early Christian movement.

Paul, a Hellenistic Jew from Tarsus, was residing in Jerusalem. The conflict around Stephen seems to have mainly involved other Hellenistic Jews in Jerusalem, belonging to "the synagogue of the Freedmen . . . Cyrenians, Alexandrians, and others of those from Cilicia and Asia" (Acts 6:9). Bear in mind that Paul was one of those Jews who had come from Cilicia. Stephen's Greek name and the views attributed to him in his long speech in Acts 7 indicate that he, too, was a Hellenistic Jew. And Stephen (and others like him) had become part of the early Christian movement. In Acts 6:5, Stephen is described as "a man full of faith and the Holy Spirit."

According to Acts 6:8–15, Stephen's opponents charged that he spoke "blasphemous words against Moses and God." These charges are made more specific when "false witnesses" claim that Stephen "never stops saying things against this holy place [the Jerusalem temple] and the law [the Mosaic Law]," and quote him as stating that "Jesus of Nazareth will destroy this place and will change the customs that Moses handed on to us" (13–14). In other words, Stephen's adherence to the Jesus movement led him and other Hellenistic Jews to question the ultimate value of the Jerusalem temple and the Mosaic Law. Thus it appears that the controversy that led Paul to become a persecutor of the

Christians was primarily based in one segment of the Jewish population in Jerusalem, that is, among the Hellenistic Jews from the Diaspora.

It is easy to see how attitudes like those of Stephen might have developed among Diaspora Jews. They lived far from the Jerusalem temple and could make the required pilgrimages infrequently and not without inconvenience. Also, they were living in a pagan, Greco-Roman cultural environment, with little support for the practices that made Jews different: circumcision, Sabbath observance, avoidance of certain foods, ritual purity rules, and so on. These were some of the factors that drew Paul and other Diaspora Jews to Jerusalem in the first place—they wanted to live a fuller Jewish life.

It appears that Stephen had found what he was looking for in Jesus of Nazareth, and had decided that the Jerusalem temple and the Mosaic Law were not so important anymore. Paul thought otherwise. According to Acts, Paul not only participated (if only as a coat holder—see 7:58) in the stoning of Stephen but also was ravaging the church in Jerusalem and dragging both men and women off to prison (8:2–3). In Acts 26:10–11, he claims that he had locked up and killed "many of the saints" in Jerusalem. He also notes that he sought and received an official commission from the Jewish high priest who gave him "letters to the synagogues at Damascus, so that if he found any who belonged to the Way, men or women, he might bring them bound to Jerusalem" (Acts 9:2; see also 22:5 and 26:12).

That Paul's persecution was focused on Hellenistic Jewish Christians is confirmed by the notice in Acts 8:2 that all the

Christians were scattered "except the apostles." Why were "the apostles" spared? This term very likely refers not only to the key Christians in Jerusalem but also to the "Hebrews" mentioned in Acts 6:1, most likely all the Palestinian Jewish Christians who spoke Hebrew (or, more likely, Aramaic) and were led by other Palestinian Jewish Christians such as Peter, James, and John. Also, in Galatians Paul says that he was "still unknown by sight to the churches of Judea" (1:22)—that is, to the Palestinian Jewish Christians. Meanwhile, the remnants of the Stephen group took refuge in Phoenicia, Cyprus, and Antioch (Acts 11:19). There they encountered non-Jews who showed great interest in their new kind of Judaism. Armed with his commission from the high priest, Paul set out for Damascus.

Paul's Conversion and Calling

Around A.D. 32 or 33 Paul, a Jew born in Tarsus of Cilicia, a Pharisee by choice, and a persecutor of Christians by conviction, underwent a remarkable transformation. What happened to Paul can be called a "conversion," at least in the sense that he moved from Pharisaic Judaism to Christian Judaism. This life-changing experience also involved a call to proclaim Christ to those who had not heard of him, especially to non-Jews.

In Galatians 1:15–16 Paul describes his transformative experience of the risen Christ partly to defend the divine origin of his apostleship: "But when God, who had set me apart before I was born and called me through his grace, was pleased to reveal his Son to me, so that I might proclaim him among the Gentiles . . ."

By evoking the language of Jeremiah 1:5 (". . . before was I born and called me . . ."), Paul places his experience in line with the Old Testament stories of people being called by God (Abraham, Moses, David, Isaiah, Jeremiah, Ezekiel, and so on) and also insists that his experience involved the special vocation of bringing the good news to non-Jews. Paul maintains that his apostleship and his call to bring the gospel to Gentiles came directly from "Jesus Christ and God the Father" (Galatians 1:1). Only later did Paul confer with the Jerusalem apostles (Galatians 1:18; 2:1), who in turn approved his calling to "go to the Gentiles" (2:9).

In Philippians 3, in response to the attacks on his apostleship by other Jewish Christian missionaries, Paul observes that this experience had changed his perspective entirely: "I regard every-thing as loss because of the surpassing value of knowing Christ Jesus my Lord" (3:8). In light of this experience, Paul's sole desire became knowing "Christ and the power of his resurrection and the sharing of his sufferings by becoming like him in his death" (3:10). This is the heart of Paul's spirituality. It involves a kind of mysticism well expressed by Paul himself: "It is no longer I who live, but it is Christ who lives in me" (Galatians 2:20).

Paul's brief autobiographical references to his "conversion" are paralleled by three much more elaborate accounts of the event in Acts 9:1–19; 22:3–21; and 26:9–18. Biblical scholars have long debated the origin and accuracy of Luke's versions. Did Luke get them directly from Paul? Or are they largely the product of Luke's own religious imagination? Rather than getting bogged down in this complex debate, I suggest that we take Paul's own statements as a reliable criterion for what happened, and judge the accounts in Acts according to their conformity with them.

Paul's confession that he had persecuted the church of God violently (Galatians 1:13) is a prominent theme in all three accounts in Acts (especially 26:9–11), and it's hardly the kind of thing that early Christians would have invented about him. His boast to have reached an advanced stage in Judaism and to have been very zealous (Galatians 1:14) is paralleled in Acts 22:3 and 26:4–5. The connection between the conversion of Paul and his mission to preach the gospel to the Gentiles is drawn in both Galatians 1:16 and Acts 26:16. Finally, Galatians 1:17 ("and afterwards I returned to Damascus") connects the incident with Damascus, though we are not told that it occurred on the way to Damascus, as in Acts. There are certainly enough similarities between Paul's statements and the three accounts in Acts to conclude that the accounts in Acts reflect some good historical traditions going back to Paul's personal experience.

Paul the Missionary

Paul was not the first Christian missionary. Early missionary activity was based to some extent on Jesus' own practice. Jesus was a traveling teacher who invited even outcasts to share in God's kingdom. He enlisted disciples and sent them out to extend his mission (see Mark 6:6b–13 and parallels). The missionary activity of the first Christians was rooted in the commission of the risen Jesus (Matthew 28:16–20; Luke 24:47). It involved the witness of Jesus' disciples "in Jerusalem, in all Judea and Samaria, and to the ends of the earth" (Acts 1:8).

At Antioch, Hellenistic Jewish Christians expelled from Jerusalem came into contact with Gentiles who surprisingly "became believers and turned to the Lord" (Acts 11:21). Thus the Christian mission to non-Jews was already in operation before Paul came upon the public scene, and Christianity was soon spreading across the Roman Empire to Rome itself (though the number of converts remained relatively small).

The spread of Christianity outside of Palestine and through the Mediterranean world was facilitated by the steady growth of the Roman Empire and the external conditions that accompanied it. The peace imposed by the Romans (*pax Romana*) made travel relatively safe by ridding the roads of bandits and the sea of pirates. The improved road system and the Roman dominance of the Mediterranean made east-to-west journeys more feasible, though not necessarily easy (2 Corinthians 11:25–28). The common language in the cities of the Roman Empire was Greek, and Paul was well trained in it.

The great cities of the Roman Empire—such as Alexandria, Antioch, Ephesus, and Rome—had large Jewish populations, and early Christianity came to them through Jewish Christians and took root in the local Jewish communities. The synagogue was the "gathering place" and local cultural center as well as the site for worshiping the God of Israel. Monotheism, high ethical standards, and frequent communal celebrations attracted non-Jews to the synagogue. Some became Jews, while many others remained in a less formal association as "God fearers." This development helps to explain how Paul, even when writing to Gentile Christians, could presume that they possessed a good knowledge of Judaism and its Scriptures.

The workplace and the household were also crucial to the spread of early Christianity. Paul was a "tentmaker" or leather worker (Acts 18:3), and his presence in the workplace made it possible for him to meet new people and exchange ideas about philosophy and religion. The Roman Empire featured many voluntary associations based on trade, religion, philosophy, or some other common interest. Such groups often met in the private homes of members wealthy enough to accommodate a fairly large number of guests. Depending on the group, the wife of the owner might play a prominent role in organizing and overseeing the gatherings.

The ten years between Paul's conversion and the letters and accounts of his missionary activity in Acts remain obscure. Paul says that he first "went away at once into Arabia, and afterwards I returned to Damascus" (Galatians 1:17), and then after his first visit to Jerusalem he went into "the regions of Syria and Cilicia" (1:21). Whether he engaged in direct missionary activity or in some kind of spiritual formation (or both), we do not know for sure. But from roughly A.D. 46 on, we have solid evidence from his letters and the book of Acts that Paul traveled about the Mediterranean world, fulfilling his call to be the apostle to the Gentiles.

Detailed information about Paul's missionary travels throughout the Mediterranean world between A.D. 46 and 58 appears in the Acts of the Apostles. Modern readers of Acts have

divided Paul's missionary career into three journeys or phases:
Acts 13:1—14:28 (A.D. 46–49); 15:30—18:17 (A.D. 50–52); and
18:18—21:16 (A.D. 54–58). The geographical scope of these jour-
neys is breathtaking, with stops at Cyprus, Antioch of Pisidia,
Iconium, Lystra and Derbe, Antioch in Syria, Jerusalem, Philippi,
Thessalonica, Beroea, Athens, Corinth, Antioch in Syria again,
Ephesus, Macedonia and Greece, Troas, Miletus, Ephesus again,
Jerusalem again, and Rome. Luke shows how Paul fulfilled the
mandate of the risen Christ about the apostles being witnesses to
"the ends of the earth" (Acts 1:8).

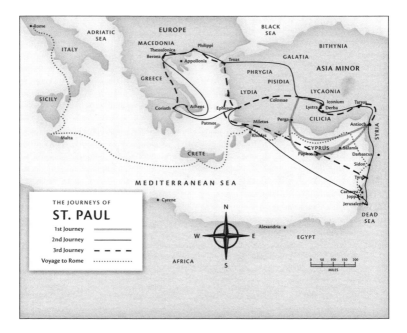

Paul did get to Rome but not in the way he envisioned in Romans 15:14–29. He had hoped to visit Rome on his way to Spain, where he was to begin a new mission in what to people of the Mediterranean world was indeed "the ends of the earth." But as he was bringing the proceeds of the collection from the Gentile Christian churches of Asia Minor and Greece to the "mother church" in Jerusalem, Paul was arrested (Acts 21:27–36), imprisoned at Caesarea Maritima, and eventually sent off to Rome, where according to Christian tradition he died a martyr's death, probably in A.D. 67, toward the end of Nero's persecution of the Christians at Rome. Whether Paul ever got to Spain is not clear. In Acts 28 Luke's story of Paul's missionary activity breaks off abruptly, with Paul in prison or under house arrest at Rome but still entertaining inquirers about Christianity and "proclaiming the, kingdom of God and teaching about the Lord Jesus Christ with all boldness and without hindrance" (28:31).

The Chronology of Paul's Life

The precise or absolute chronology of Paul's life as a Christian is not easy to discern, with various learned scholars proposing different dates for where Paul was and what he was doing. The two instances of relatively "hard data" providing exact dating in his letters to the Galatians turn out to cause as many problems as they solve. According to Galatians 1:18, Paul went up to Jerusalem for the first time as a Christian only "after three years," presumably after his transformative experience of the risen Christ. If we leave some time for Paul's activity as a persecutor of Christians after Jesus' death, that would put Paul's conversion around A.D. 32 or 33. Then his first visit to Jerusalem as a Christian would have been in 35 or 36.

In Galatians 2:1 Paul says that "after fourteen years I went up again to Jerusalem." Was that fourteen years after his first visit, or fourteen years after his conversion? The latter seems more likely, and that would place the second visit and the Jerusalem conference or council (see Galatians 2:1–10; Acts 15) in 47 or 48. Between his second visit to Jerusalem and his long stay at Corinth, Paul had his famous confrontation with Peter in Antioch in 48 or 49 over the propriety of Jewish and Gentile Christians eating together (Galatians 2:11–14).

According to Acts 18:11, Paul then stayed at Corinth for a year and six months. There Paul wrote his first extant letter, 1 Thessalonians, to one of the communities he had founded. According to 18:12, Gallio was proconsul of Achaia when the local Jewish leaders attacked Paul and brought him before the tribunal there. From an inscription found at Delphi in 1905 we know that Gallio served there between 51 and 52. So Paul must have spent time at Corinth in 50–51 (or 51–52).

Following a return to Antioch, Paul settled down in Ephesus for a period of about two years (53–55), with side-trips else-where. While there he wrote the letters known as Galatians and 1 Corinthians. Many scholars suppose that while in Ephesus Paul suffered another imprisonment (2 Corinthians 1:8–11) not mentioned in Acts, during which he wrote his prison letters to the Philippians and Philemon. He seems to have written 2 Corinthians (or parts of it) while in Macedonia. During another stay in Corinth he wrote his letter to the Romans in the year 56 or 57.

While bringing the proceeds of the collection taken up among the Gentile churches for the "poor" Christians at Jerusalem, Paul was arrested and imprisoned in 57 in Caesarea Maritima in Palestine, off the Mediterranean coast. From there he was taken by ship in 58 to Rome for trial, on the grounds that he was a Roman citizen and deserved a trial befitting his legal status. In Rome he was in prison or under house arrest from 58 onward. According to later Christian tradition, Paul was executed under the emperor Nero sometime in the mid- to late 60s of the first century.

Paul the Partner in Ministry

The concept of collaborative ministry in the church is not a late twentieth-century invention. Rather, the earliest complete documents in the New Testament—Paul's letters from the 50s of the first century—show that the Christian mission was collaborative from the beginning. Paul, the great apostle to the Gentiles, worked as part of a team of Christians.

Both in his missionary travels and in his local pastoral activities, Paul depended on a network of friends and associates. Paul did not work alone. In fact, his frequent use of the Greek word for "coworker" (*synergos*) is the biblical basis for talk about "collaborative" (the Latin-based equivalent) ministry today. Paul bestowed the title *synergos* on the following persons:

> Timothy (1 Thessalonians 3:2; Romans 16:21)
> Philemon (Philemon 1)
> Mark, Aristarchus, Demas, and Luke
>   (Philemon 24)
> Epaphroditus (Philippians 2:25)
> Eudoia, Syntyche, Clement, and others
>   (Philippians 4:2–3)
> Apollos (1 Corinthians 3:5–9)
> Titus (2 Corinthians 8:23)
> (perhaps) Stephanus, Fortunatus, and Achaicus (1
>   Corinthians 16:17)
> Prisca and Aquila (Romans 16:3)
> Urbanus (Romans 16:9)

Related expressions are applied to Mary in Romans 16:6 ("who has worked hard among you") and to Tryphaena and Tryphosa in Romans 16:12 ("those workers in the Lord").

Paul is best described as a pastoral theologian. His letters provided advice on being a Christian to the early communities, and he developed his theology mainly in the process of giving this pastoral advice. Because Paul's advice was so sound and inspiring, his letters eventually became part of the canon of Christian Scripture, and he is justly celebrated as one of the greatest theologians ever. Nevertheless, apart from Galatians and Romans, all the undisputed Pauline letters are identified as jointly authored compositions:

Paul, Silvanus, and Timothy (1 Thessalonians)
Paul and Timothy (Philemon, Philippians,
    2 Corinthians)
Paul and Sosthenes (1 Corinthians)

Even though in the main text Paul often speaks in the first person singular ("I"), his letters presumably also were shared by his coworkers and represented their views as well.

The communities that Paul founded gathered in the houses of certain well-to-do members who could host assemblies of up to forty or fifty persons. In fact, without the householder's consent and some organization by community members, there wouldn't have been local community gatherings. Paul's letter to his "coworker" Philemon is also addressed to "the church in your house." The implication is that Paul intended that the letter would be read publicly to the community based at the home of Philemon and Apphia. In this short letter, part of Paul's strategy was to persuade (or shame?) Philemon to take back into his household his runaway slave Onesimus as "a beloved brother."

Before Paul's letters from the 50s of the first century, Christians had already developed faith statements about Jesus (1 Corinthians 15:3–5; Philippians 2:6–11; Romans 1:3–4; 3:25), the rituals of baptism and the Lord's Supper, and ethical teachings. It is enough to read Paul's earliest letter (1 Thessalonians) written some twenty years after Jesus' death, to recognize the linguistic, conceptual, and theological "explosion" that took place in the earliest days of the Christian movement. In his ministry and writings Paul was able to build upon these established beliefs and practices, and in many cases to provide theological depth for them.

Paul's Motivations

Paul took up his missionary practice out of a strong sense of vocation. His conversion experience of the risen Christ was for him also a call to proclaim Christ among the Gentiles (Galatians 1:16). That experience was so profound that Paul felt himself mystically identified with Christ: "it is no longer I who live, but it is Christ who lives in me" (Galatians 2:20). Paul was convinced that his spiritual gift (or charism) was to be an apostle, one sent to proclaim the gospel (Galatians 1:1), especially to non-Jews. Paul's ultimate hope was to know Christ and to share in his sufferings and resurrection so as to "attain the resurrection from the dead" (Philippians 3:10–11).

In the midst of his apostolic activity, however, Paul did not lose sight of the fact that he was always acting as God's servant. In response to members of factions at Corinth who boasted about the different apostles who had brought them to Christian faith, Paul condemned their bickering, on the grounds that Cephas (Peter), Apollos, Paul, and all the other apostles were merely servants of God and Christ. In 1 Corinthians 3, Paul uses the analogies of caring for a plant and constructing a building to show that in the Christian mission God gives the growth and Christ is the real foundation (3:11). There Paul reminds the Corinthians (and us) that "we are God's servants, working together; you are God's field, God's building" (3:9).

Paul's own stated policy (Romans 15:14–29) was to proclaim the good news of Christ to non-Jews in places where there was no church and where the gospel had not yet been preached (15:20). He took care not to build on anyone else's foundation. And when Paul perceived that the new local church was "up and running," he moved on to a new site.

Christianity had come to Rome through the local Jewish community, long before Paul arrived there. This fact explains the tone of the thanksgiving (1:8–15) in Paul's letter to the Romans. Paul knew well that Christianity was already established in Rome. And so he presented his planned visit as merely a stopover on his way to the western edge of the Mediterranean world: "I will set out by way of you to Spain" (15:28). In other words, one of Paul's purposes in writing his long letter to the Romans was to request hospitality on his way to Spain. He hoped that his stay there might be an occasion for sharing spiritual gifts (1:11–12). While undertaking his pioneering mission, Paul was nevertheless deeply intertwined with and dependent upon other Christians.

The Role of Paul's Letters

Of the seven letters generally acknowledged to have been written by Paul himself (1 Thessalonians, Galatians, Philippians, Philemon, 1 and 2 Corinthians, and Romans), all but Romans were sent to communities that Paul had founded. These letters were intended primarily as extensions of Paul's own missionary activity. They provided advice, encouragement, and correction from the founding apostle in his physical absence.

In writing to these communities, Paul followed the conventions of letter-writing in the Greco-Roman world at that time. The opening or salutation identified the writer and the addressee by name, and included a greeting ("grace," or "peace" in the Jewish tradition). This was generally followed by words of remembrance and thanksgiving for past favors and wishes for good health and prosperity in the present and future. The body of the letter dealt with the major topics and concerns that had led the writer to compose the letter. At the end of the letter there might be personal greetings, more good wishes, news about travel plans, and a final benediction.

Most of the Pauline letters follow this outline, though always there are adaptations that serve to "Christianize" the pattern and to respond to the circumstances of the local community. For example, in identifying himself Paul often expands upon his call to be an apostle (Galatians 1:1), and uses the thanksgiving as the occasion to introduce the main themes to be developed in the body of the letters. And in Galatians, Paul was so incensed that he omitted the thanksgiving entirely and got right down to the business of correcting the situation among the Galatian Christians.

Paul's letters were "occasional" writings—that is, Paul wrote them in response to specific events or problems within the Christian communities. In them Paul applied theological insights to the issues that had arisen in these congregations.

The letters were intended to be (and most certainly were) read publicly to the whole community. So prized were these letters that early Christians saved them, copied them, and began to put them together in packets or collections. Eventually these packets began to circulate among the different communities, even those not directly addressed by Paul. This process may well have initiated the development of the New Testament canon of Sacred Scripture alongside what had been the earliest Christians' biblical canon, what we now call the Old Testament. By the late second century the four Gospels, Acts, and the Pauline epistles had become the core of the emerging New Testament canon.

In editions of the Christian Bible it has become customary to arrange the thirteen Pauline epistles into two groups: those addressed to communities, and those addressed to individuals. Within these two groups the individual letters are arranged by length, from the longer to the shorter. Thus the nine letters addressed to communities are Romans, 1 Corinthians, 2 Corinthians, Galatians, Ephesians, Philippians, Colossians, 1 Thessalonians, and 2 Thessalonians. The four letters addressed to individuals are 1 Timothy, 2 Timothy, Titus, and Philemon.

While all thirteen letters are attributed to Paul in some way or other (several are presented as joint compositions), many modern scholars have argued that six out of the thirteen letters may have been written in Paul's name by students or admirers of Paul, most likely after Paul's death. These letters are called the "Deuteropaulines" or secondary Pauline letters.

The Deuteropaulines are certainly part of the Christian canon of Holy Scripture. While their authenticity is not at stake, their authorship by Paul is questioned on several accounts. Their language and style are often somewhat different from those of the undisputed letters of Paul. They may reflect problems and conditions within the churches later in the first century than the undisputed letters do. And they show different theological emphases and concerns from what we find in the earlier letters.

The practice of imitating, updating, and expanding model compositions as a way of learning how to write various literary forms and in various literary styles was common in the schools of the Greco-Roman world. Moreover, it is likely that a Pauline "school" developed, most likely at Ephesus, after Paul's death. Perhaps by preserving fragments written directly by Paul, these Deuteropauline letters try to tell us what Paul *would have said* in response to changing conditions and concerns that developed in the late first century.

Not all scholars have been convinced by these arguments. They point out the complex process by which the Pauline letters were written. In several of the undisputed letters Paul clearly used the services of a scribe or secretary. In Romans 16:22, one of them even steps out of his role and sends his personal greetings from Corinth to his Christian friends at Rome: "I Tertius, the writer of this letter, greet you in the Lord." How much freedom was allowed to such a scribe makes the argument about language and style not as strong as it might appear at first sight. Not only that, several of the letters are presented as joint compositions by Paul and other coworkers, which raises the question as to how much influence these other persons exercised in the composition of the letters. We should remember, however, that

Paul immediately shifts into first-person singular language rather quickly in most of these jointly authored letters. Of course, one can argue (as most earlier interpreters did) that Paul's theology and style changed and developed as he grew older, and so the Deuteropaulines can be read as reflecting Paul's mature thinking on matters that he confronted during his later years.

I find convincing the arguments for distinguishing between the undisputed Pauline letters (1 Thessalonians, Galatians, Philippians, Philemon, 1 and 2 Corinthians, and Romans) and the Deuteropauline letters (2 Thessalonians, Colossians, Ephesians, 1 and 2 Timothy, and Titus). Therefore I will treat them in two separate chapters. In the undisputed letters we will meet Paul the apostle and letter writer firsthand. In the Deuteropauline letters we will encounter the legacy or influence of Paul the apostle and letter writer. From both groups of letters we can learn much about Paul and the early Christian movement that he did so much to strengthen and spread. And of course, both groups of letters are part of sacred Scripture for Christians.

2

What Do We Learn from Paul's Letters?

The seven letters covered in this chapter are regarded by almost all biblical scholars as written directly by Paul, though some letters claim to be joint compositions and Paul seems to have used the services of a secretary from time to time (Romans 16:22). They are thus the very best sources for understanding Paul's person, his career as an apostle, and his theology. The letters are treated in their rough chronological order in Paul's career.

The First Letter to the Thessalonians (A.D. 50 or 51)

The Letter to the Galatians (A.D. 53 or 54)

The First Letter to the Corinthians (A.D. 54 or 55)

The Letter to the Philippians (A.D. 54 or 55)

The Letter to Philemon (A.D. 54 or 55)

The Second Letter to the Corinthians (A.D. 54 or 55)

The Letter to the Romans (A.D. 56 or 57)

But we do not want you to be uninformed, brothers and sisters, about those who have died, so that you may not grieve as others do who have no hope. For since we believe that Jesus died and rose again, even so, through Jesus, God will bring with him those who have died. For this we declare to you by the word of the Lord, that we who are alive, who are left until the coming of the Lord, will by no means precede those who have died. For the Lord himself, with a call and with the sound of God's trumpet, will descend from heaven, and the dead in Christ will rise first. Then we who are alive, who are left, will be caught up in the clouds together with them to meet the Lord in the air; and so we will be with the Lord forever. Therefore encourage one another with these words.

—1 Thessalonians 4:13–18

The First Letter to the Thessalonians

According to Acts 17:1–10, Paul and Silas brought the gospel to Thessalonica in northern Greece. They first preached "the Messiah Jesus" in the local synagogue. While some Jews accepted their preaching, Paul and Silas had greater success among the local Gentile population. All of this angered the local Jewish community whose leaders described the apostles as "turning the world upside down" (17:6). And so Paul and Silas were forced to flee by night.

When Paul arrived in Athens, he sent Timothy to visit the Thessalonian Christians and to report back to Paul on the state of their community. Paul, Silvanus (Silas), and Timothy wrote 1 Thessalonians as a follow-up to Timothy's visit and report. Paul was in Corinth at the time of its writing, and the letter is usually dated to A.D. 50 or 51. This letter to the Thessalonian church is the earliest complete document in the New Testament.

While the greeting (1:1) indicates joint authorship, Paul quickly assumes the role of primary speaker. He shows great affection for his converts and praises them for the faith, love, and hope they have displayed. His description of them as having turned "to God from idols, to serve a living and true God" (1:9) suggests that the audience for the letter was predominantly (if not exclusively) Gentile.

Paul seems to have been satisfied from Timothy's report that the Thessalonian Christians were making good progress. And so his main purpose in the letter was to affirm and encourage them to even greater progress in their new faith. But Timothy also appears to have noted some confusion at Thessalonica regarding the second coming of Jesus and the fate of those Christians who might die before it happened. In 1 Thessalonians 4:13—5:11

Paul insists that those believers who die before Jesus' return will indeed participate in the glorious coming of the Lord. In the meantime, he urges constant watchfulness and righteous action as the best preparations for God's definitive, or final, judgment on humankind.

This letter shows us that distinctively Christian concepts and theological language had developed very rapidly in the twenty years between Jesus' death (in A.D. 30) and Paul's letter (in A.D. 50 or 51). While some terms and ideas can be traced to the Greek Old Testament (Septuagint) and to Roman imperial propaganda (the emperor as a deity), it is remarkable that Jesus of Nazareth was already being celebrated as "the Lord Jesus Christ" and that the Christians had such lively expectations about his glorious second coming.

This letter also illustrates many of the literary characteristics that became standard in the various letters associated with Paul:

> the opening or greeting
> the thanksgiving
> the doctrinal and ethical advice as the body of the
>   letter
> travel plans, personal greetings, etc.

Near the end of the text, Paul directs that this letter be read aloud to the local community: "I solemnly command you by the Lord that this letter be read to all of them" (5:27). He clearly intended the letter to provide pastoral advice for the whole community, not just for an inner circle of church leaders.

Overview of 1 Thessalonians

Opening (1:1)

Faith (1:2—2:12)

    Thanksgiving for the community's good
condition (1:2–10)

    Remembrance of Paul's presence in
Thessalonica (2:1–12)

Love (2:13—4:12)

    Thanksgiving for the community's
steadfastness (2:13–16)

    Timothy's mission and report to Paul
(2:17—3:10)

    Prayer for the community (3:11–13)

    Exhortation to holiness and love (4:1–12)

Hope (4:13—5:22)

    The coming of the Lord and those who have
died (4:13–18)

    Exhortation to prepare for the day of the
Lord (5:1–11)

    Exhortation about ongoing community life
(5:12–22)

Closing (5:23–28)

Major Themes of This Letter

Paul the Apostle. First Thessalonians provides a glimpse into the
warm personal relationship that existed between Paul the founding

apostle and the Thessalonian Christians. He compares himself to a "nurse tenderly caring for her own children" (2:7) and to a "father with his children" (2:11). What makes their relationship Christian is their common commitment to the gospel of God. Paul attributes their reception of that gospel as due not to his own person or word but rather to "God's word, which is also at work in you believers" (2:13). That word is living and effective, exercising its own dynamism and bringing together all who believe and accept it. Paul is at best the minister or instrument of that word.

The letter is both a substitute for and an extension of Paul's personal presence among the Thessalonians. It allowed Paul, then some distance away in Corinth, to continue encouraging his converts and to clarify some misunderstandings, especially those about the second coming of Jesus. Paul's sending of Timothy to the Thessalonians, and Timothy's subsequent report about that visit, illustrate that Paul understood himself as part of a network or team of Christian missionaries. Finally, his prayers and good wishes for the community (1:2–10; 2:13–16; 3:11–13; 5:23–28) show that what gave energy to the early church was their common faith, love, and hope in "God the Father and the Lord Jesus Christ" (1:1).

Ethical Teachings. What makes Paul's ethical instructions in 4:1–12 and 5:12–22 rise above the level of typical Greco-Roman morals is that their context is Christ-like living. These wise teachings have been adapted and integrated into what Paul and other early Christian teachers used to shape their understanding of Christian character and appropriate behavior "in the Lord Jesus" (4:1). Indeed the Christian theological virtues mentioned in the opening thanksgiving ("your work of faith and labor of love and steadfastness of hope," 1:3) seem to serve as structure for the entire letter (as my outline suggests).

Christ's Second Coming. On the theological level, 1 Thessalonians is most famous for its description of Jesus' glorious second coming in 4:13–18. That description is unusually concrete and even fantastic, more like what one might find in Jewish apocalyptic writings. However, Paul's basic point is to affirm that believers who had died already will participate in that event (1 Corinthians 15:50–57). And in 5:1–11 Paul quickly dampened the Thessalonians' enthusiasm about end-times events by insisting that since the precise time of Christ's return is unknown (Mark 13:32), the proper Christian attitude is constant vigilance and behavior appropriate to those who seek to obtain "salvation through our Lord Jesus Christ" (5:9). Paul's description of those who will witness the second coming ("we who are alive, who are left, will be caught up in the clouds" 4:17) suggests that he may well have expected it to happen soon, in his own lifetime.

Key Texts and Questions

Read 1 Thessalonians 2:1–13. What did being an apostle mean to Paul?

Read 4:13–18. How is the Christian to think about death?

Read 5:1–10. How does belief in Christ's second coming influence the way you live today?

The fruit of the Spirit is love, joy, peace, patience, kindness, generosity, faithfulness, gentleness, and self-control. There is no law against such things. And those who belong to Christ Jesus have crucified the flesh with its passions and desires. If we live by the Spirit, let us also be guided by the Spirit.

—Galatians 5:22–25

The Letter to the Galatians

Paul's letter to the Galatians is most famous for its doctrine of justification by faith and its defense of Christian freedom. However, it was composed not so much as a theological argument as it was written in response to a crisis in the churches of Galatia. The "churches of Galatia" that it addresses were in central Asia Minor (in the general vicinity of Ankara in modern Turkey). The Galatians were people of Celtic origin, the descendants of mercenaries who had settled there in the third and second centuries B.C. Paul brought these people to Christian faith, most likely during his second and third missionary journeys (Acts 16:6; 18:23).

The Galatian Christians were Gentiles, which set them apart from other groups of believers who were primarily Jews. We must keep in mind that the original followers of Jesus came out of his own Jewish community, and that there continued to be hesitance on the part of Jewish believers to welcome people outside their community. The evangelization of such people as the Galatians was part of Paul's special calling to proclaim Christ "among the Gentiles" (1:16). Paul insisted that these people did not have to observe the Mosaic Law—something that naturally was very important to Jews who became followers of Jesus and who saw no reason to abandon their faith tradition, including the Law of Moses. Paul was convinced that Gentile believers were already in right relationship with God ("justified") through their faith in Christ, and that they had already received the Holy Spirit without being circumcised and observing the Mosaic Law (3:1–5). From Paul's perspective, there was no need for them to become Jews in order to be full members of God's people in Christ.

However, it appears that after Paul had moved on, a rival group of Jewish Christian missionaries arrived in the churches of Galatia and were telling the Galatian Christians that in order to be real Christians they must be circumcised and must observe the entire Jewish Law, including Sabbath, food, and ritual purity regulations. They apparently reasoned that since Jesus is the Messiah of Israel, only those believers in him who were Jews or who *became* Jews could enjoy the benefits of Jesus and his teachings. These missionaries were effectively casting doubt on Paul—the founding apostle of the churches in Galatia—and on the message he had preached there.

Paul wrote his letter to the churches of Galatia to clear up the doubt and confusion that the rival Jewish Christian missionaries had caused. He wrote the letter most likely around A.D. 53 or 54 in Ephesus. In the opening greeting (1:1–3) Paul insists that his apostleship came directly "through Jesus Christ and God the Father," and that the Lord Jesus Christ "gave himself for our sins to set us free from the present evil age." In other words, the gospel that Paul preached was the good news that Jesus' death and resurrection had made it possible to be in right relationship with God (justification), something that circumcision and observance of the Mosaic Law could never do.

Paul's basic thesis in his letter to the Galatians is expressed in 2:16: "yet we know that a person is justified not by the works of the law but through faith in Jesus Christ." In developing this proposition Paul appeals first to his own call from the risen Christ to proclaim this good news to non-Jews, and then to the approval that his gospel and mission had received from the leaders of the church in Jerusalem—from Peter, James, and John (2:9). Next he demonstrates his skill in interpreting the Jewish Scriptures by showing that people of faith who belong to Christ are the real children of Abraham (3:27–29). Then he urges the Gentile Christians at Galatia not to trade their Christian freedom for the servitude that would come with accepting circumcision and observing the Mosaic Law. Already living in right relationship with God and endowed with the gifts of the Holy Spirit, the Galatian Christians actually were fulfilling the deepest and soundest *intentions* of the Mosaic law. For them circumcision was at best a matter of indifference (6:15) and at worst a sign of enslavement to the power of sin, death, and the Law.

Overview of Galatians
Opening (1:1–5)
The truth of the gospel (1:6—4:31)
No other gospel (1:6–10)
Historical arguments (1:11—2:14)
Paul's gospel (1:11–12)
His former life and call (1:13–17)
First visit to Jerusalem (1:18–24)
Second visit to Jerusalem (2:1–10)
The Antioch incident (2:11–14)
Biblical and theological arguments
(2:15—4:31)
Paul's gospel (2:15–21)
The Galatians' experience (3:1–5)
Abraham's faith (3:6–9)

Overview of Galatians, cont.

Freedom from the curse of the Law
(3:10–14)

Abraham and the promise (3:15–18)

The purpose of the Law (3:19–26)

The true descendants of Abraham
(3:27–29)

The sending of the Son (4:1–7)

The Galatians' experience (4:8–20)

The allegory of Hagar and Sarah
(4:21–31)

Christian freedom (5:1—6:10)

The nature of freedom (5:1–15)

Works of the flesh and fruit of the Spirit
(5:16–26)

Exhortation on community life (6:1–10)

Closing (6:11–18)

Paul's personal remarks (6:11–17)

Closing benediction (6:18)

Major Themes of This Letter

Paul's Christ-Mysticism. Paul never met the earthly Jesus. Yet his experience of the risen Jesus was so powerful that it developed in him what can be described as a mystical experience of Christ. This is best expressed in 2:20: "and it is no longer I who live, but it is Christ who lives in me." At the heart of Paul's Christ-mysticism was the mystery of Jesus' death and resurrection. His parting comment in 6:17 ("for I carry the marks of Jesus branded on my body") has for centuries fueled speculation that Paul bore the actual wounds (*stigmata*) of Christ on his body. Even if Paul intended his remark merely as a metaphor, it does underline how central the cross of Christ was in Paul's experience of Christ.

Paul's description of his experience of the risen Christ in 1:13–17 is the most significant conversion story in Christian history. Paul, the proud Pharisee and zealous persecutor of the Christian movement, was transformed into the most enthusiastic and persistent champion of the significance of Jesus' death and resurrection. It is important to note, however, that Paul most likely perceived his "conversion" as moving from one kind of Judaism (Pharisaism) to another (Christianity). In other words, Paul found the fullness of Judaism in and through Christ. Not only that, but the call that Paul received to proclaim Christ among the Gentiles was integral to his experience of conversion. This was not merely a mystical experience aimed at personal fulfillment; it was an inner transformation that immediately moved outward, toward the spiritual well-being of others.

Faith in/of Christ. In Galatians (2:16 [twice]; 2:20; 3:22) and elsewhere, Paul uses the Greek phrase *pistis tou Christou*. That phrase can be translated either as "the faith of Christ" or as "faith *in* Christ." In the first use of this term, Paul is referring to the faithfulness or trust displayed by Jesus toward his heavenly Father and his fellow humans. In the second use, Christ is the object of faith, and "faith in Christ" becomes the way by which we can enter into new life. The *New Revised Standard Version* (NRSV) of the Bible generally places the objective reading in the main text and refers to the subjective reading as another possibility in a note below.

Arguing from Scripture. In his argument against the other Jewish Christian missionaries, Paul's use of Scripture would have had a special significance. In Galatians 3 (and elsewhere) Paul shows himself to be adept at constructing a theological argument on the basis of various biblical texts, a tactic he may well have learned in his training as a Pharisee. But for him, Christ had become the key that opens up the mysteries of the Scriptures. Paul wants to show that people of faith (in Christ) are the true children of Abraham, and that therefore there is no need for Gentile Christians to become Jews.

A look at the beginning of Paul's argument (3:6–14) can illustrate Paul's method. Taking Genesis 15:6 as the starting point, Paul says in 3:6 that Abraham "believed God, and it was reckoned to him as righteousness." The pattern of *justification by faith* is applied to all people of faith so that they constitute the children of Abraham (3:6–7). To confirm his thesis, Paul weaves a web of biblical quotations and personal comments. In 3:8 he cites Genesis 12:3 (or 18:18) to the effect that all the nations are blessed in Abraham, and adds in 3:9 that faith is the means by which this blessing is received. Then he uses Deuteronomy 27:26 to argue that those who rely on the works of the Law are under a curse (3:10), Habakkuk 2:4 to show that we are justified by faith (3:11), Leviticus 18:5 to demonstrate that faith and the Law are at odds with each other (3:12), and Deuteronomy 21:23 to affirm that Christ has redeemed us from the curse of the law (3:13). All these texts lead to Paul's basic conclusion in 3:14: "that in Christ Jesus the blessing of Abraham might come to the Gentiles, so that we might receive the promise of the Spirit through faith."

The Mosaic Law. Why then do we have the Law? When Paul uses the Greek word *nomos* ("law"), he is generally (but not always) referring to the Mosaic Law or the Torah. Essential to Paul's argument in Galatians is the idea that observance of the Law cannot do what Christ's death and resurrection have done—that is, bring about right relationship with God (justification).

In 3:19–26 Paul offers several ideas about God's purpose in giving us the Law of Moses if the laws themselves could not give us a right relationship with God. First, the Law was secondary to the promise made to Abraham, provisional until Christ's coming, and inferior to the promise because it was mediated through angels (3:19–20). Second, the Law was given in order to reveal the absolute necessity of grace and Christ's life, death, and resurrection as the only effective means of bringing about right relationship with God (3:21–22). Third, the Law served as a guide and guardian while we were spiritually young and needed supervision "until Christ came" (3:23–25).

Paul and Judaism. The letter to the Galatians is sometimes put forward as evidence that Paul was anti-Jewish. That might seem the case when this letter is read without any reference to the history behind it. But Paul was not anti-Jewish. He writes as a Jew convinced that he has found the fullness of Judaism in the person of Jesus Christ. Moreover, the opponents against whom he is struggling are also (like Paul) Jewish Christians. What is at stake in the Galatian church is the identity of non-Jews who become Christians. Do they need also to become Jews and observe the Law? The opponents say "Yes, they do," while Paul says "No, they don't." Even in the mysterious allegory of Hagar and Sarah in 4:21–31, it is not a matter of Jews versus Christians. Rather, the children of the slave woman (Hagar) represent Gentile Christians who might become Jews, while the children of the free woman (Sarah) represent Gentile Christians who will not do so because they do not need to.

Christian Freedom. In the second part of his letter, Paul proclaims that "for freedom Christ has set us free" (5:1). However, Paul could not envision life without a master; our present-day notion of "complete autonomy" was not part of Paul's worldview—or anyone's worldview at that time. The very title "the Lord Jesus Christ" suggests that Christ is the only master worth serving. There is a political dimension to this title, since the Greek term *kyrios* ("lord") was one of the titles of the Roman emperor. There is also a theological dimension, in that Paul was convinced that the death and resurrection of Jesus made it possible for us to escape our slavery to sin, death, and the Law, and freed us to live "in the Spirit." This idea is developed in greater detail in Romans 5—8, but it is present in Paul's letter to the Galatians.

Paul goes on to show that Christian freedom does not mean license to do anything we please. Paul freely borrows ethical teachings from the Old Testament and from the Greco-Roman moralists, which he regards as consistent with the identity of the Christian. One goal of his letters was to help in forming Christian character. He presents in 5:16–21 a list of vices or what he calls "the desires of the flesh." These are attitudes and actions that are incompatible with Christian character and the Christian's exercise of freedom. On the other hand, his list of "the fruit of the Spirit" in 5:22–23 corresponds to the virtues that are most appropriate for those who are led by the Holy Spirit. The great principle of the morality described by Paul is stated in 5:25: "If we live by the Spirit, let us also be guided by the Spirit."

Key Texts and Questions

Read Galatians 2:15–21. What does it mean to you, on a day-to-day basis, that you are "justified" by faith in Christ and not by following the Law?

Read 3:27–29. What does it mean for you to be a child of Abraham?

Read 5:16–26. What virtues and values are most appropriate for those who live by the Spirit? If you were to translate Paul's lists into today's terminology, what would they look like?

Love is patient; love is kind; love is not envious or boastful or arrogant or rude. It does not insist on its own way; it is not irritable or resentful; it does not rejoice in wrongdoing, but rejoices in the truth. It bears all things, believes all things, hopes all things, endures all things. Love never ends. But as for prophecies, they will come to an end; as for tongues, they will cease; as for knowledge, it will come to an end. For we know only in part, and we prophesy only in part; but when the complete comes, the partial will come to an end. When I was a child, I spoke like a child, I thought like a child, I reasoned like a child; when I became an adult, I put an end to childish ways. For now we see in a mirror, dimly, but then we will see face to face. Now I know only in part; then I will know fully, even as I have been fully known. And now faith, hope, and love abide, these three; and the greatest of these is love.

—1 Corinthians 13:4–13

The First Letter to the Corinthians

Corinth controlled the isthmus that linked the Greek mainland with the Peloponnesian peninsula. It played a leading role in uniting the Greek city-states in the time of Philip of Macedon and Alexander the Great. It was destroyed by the Romans in 246 B.C. because of its leadership in the effort of the Achaian League to stop Rome's expansion into Greece. It was rebuilt under Julius Caesar in 44 B.C. and became a provincial capital in 27 B.C. In Paul's time, Corinth was a thriving commercial center, largely because of its geographical position. It attracted devotees of various traditional Greek cults as well as proponents of religions from the east, including Judaism and Christianity.

According to Acts 18, Paul brought Christianity to Corinth. At first he lodged with Aquila and Prisca (called Priscilla in Acts), a Jewish Christian couple exiled from Rome under the emperor Claudius in A.D. 49. He also engaged with them in tent making or some related leather-working enterprise. Paul was eventually joined by Timothy and Silas. He had some success within the local Jewish community but also ignited fierce opposition from it. When brought for trial before the proconsul Gallio in A.D. 51, he was released unharmed because Gallio refused to become involved in what he dismissed as an inner-Jewish religious quarrel. Eventually Paul left Corinth and arrived in Ephesus, which he made his base of operations. He wrote what we call 1 Corinthians from Ephesus in the spring of A.D. 54 or 55. Paul planned to stay at Ephesus until late spring ("until Pentecost," 1 Corinthians 16:8), and hoped to visit Corinth soon thereafter (16:6).

This was not the first letter that Paul wrote to the Corinthian Christians. In 5:9 Paul claims that "I wrote to you in my letter not to associate with sexually immoral persons." In the salutation (1:1–3) Paul and Sosthenes are identified as coauthors of this letter. But in 1:4 Paul immediately shifts into first-person language. The addressees belong to "the church of God that is in Corinth." Whereas in Acts 18 the focus is on Paul's dealings with the local Jewish community, most of the issues that he takes up in 1 Corinthians seem more appropriate to Gentile Christians. While there may have been a few prominent persons among the Corinthian Christians (Romans 16:23), Paul states in 1:26 that "not many of you were wise by human standards, not many were powerful, not many were of noble birth." The Corinthian Christian community most likely had a Jewish Christian nucleus, along with many more Gentile members, from different socioeconomic levels. Tensions among the various social groups appear in many parts of the letter, but especially with regard to the celebration of the Lord's Supper (11:17–34).

First Corinthians is the clearest example of Paul the pastoral theologian at work. He addresses some problems and questions that had arisen among the Christians at Corinth. He provides theological reflections on these matters as well as practical advice. The first six chapters concern the divisions within the community as reported by "Chloe's people" (1:11) as well as cases of sexual immorality and litigiousness (5:1; 6:1). Most of the rest of the letter answers questions raised in another letter sent by the Corinthians to Paul: "Now concerning the matters about which you wrote . . ." (7:1). They include marriage and divorce, eating food sacrificed to idols, order and proper behavior in the Christian assembly and at the Lord's Supper, the spiritual gifts, and the resurrection of the dead.

It has often been said that the issues dealt with in 1 Corinthians are, in some form, the same problems that confront churches today. They include divisions, sexual immorality, the role of women, crises of conscience, liturgical abuses, pride over spiritual gifts, and lack of hope in the resurrection. If that claim has merit, we need to pay close attention to how Paul treats these problems. Perhaps more than any other Pauline letter, 1 Corinthians is most clearly a substitute for Paul's personal presence and an extension of his ministry as an apostle.

Overview of 1 Corinthians
Opening (1:1–3)
Thanksgiving (1:4–9)
Divisions in the community (1:10—4:21)
    Groups in the community (1:10–17)
    The proclamation of the cross (1:18—2:5)
    The true wisdom of God (2:6—3:4)
    Groups and the community (3:5–23)
    The apostles and their ministry (4:1–16)
    Travel plans (4:17–21)
Immorality and litigation (5:1—6:20)
    The incestuous man (5:1–13)
    Lawsuits among believers (6:1–11)
    Visiting prostitutes (6:12–20)
Marriage and related matters (7:1–40)

Overview of 1 Corinthians, cont.

    Husbands and wives (7:1–7)

    Widowers and widows (7:8–9)

    Marriage and divorce (7:10–16)

    Stay as you are! (7:17–24)

    The unmarried (7:25–38)

    Widows (7:39–40)

Food offered to idols (8:1—11:1)

    Issues and advice (8:1–13)

    Paul's example (9:1–27)

    Examples from Israel's past (10:1–13)

    More advice (10:14—11:1)

Order in Christian worship (11:2–34)

    Women and men in prayer and prophecy (11:2–16)

    The Lord's Supper (11:17–34)

Spiritual gifts (12:1—14:40)

    The variety of gifts (12:1–11)

    The body of Christ (12:12–31)

    The gift of love (13:1–13)

    The gifts of prophecy and tongues (14:1–25)

    Orderly worship (14:26–40)

Resurrection (15:1–58)

    Resurrection of Christ (15:1–11)

    Resurrection of the dead (15:12–34)

    Resurrection of the body (15:35–58)

Other matters (16:1–20)

    The collection (16:1–4)

    Travel plans (16:5–12)

Overview of 1 Corinthians, cont.
Final messages and greetings (16:13–20)
Closing (16:21–24)

Major Themes of This Letter

The Wisdom of the Cross. The first problem that Paul takes up is the presence of factions or divisions within the Christian community. It appears that various groups had gathered around the apostles who had brought them to Christian faith and perhaps baptized them. They were saying, "I belong to Paul" or "I belong to Apollos" or "I belong to Cephas." Others were saying, "I belong to Christ," perhaps as a way to trump the claims of their rivals. What seemed to be at issue was the superior spiritual wisdom that individuals within the various factions were claiming for themselves.

Rather than sorting out these disputes, taking one side against the others, or exalting himself as the greatest apostle, Paul deflates the claims of them all by appealing to the cross of Christ as the revelation of God's wisdom for humankind. He identifies the crucified Christ as "the power of God and the wisdom of God" (1:24). Thus he challenges the Corinthians to recall what was the core of their faith when they became Christians and to take the cross of Christ as the true wisdom of God and the criterion for all other kinds of wisdom.

In 3:1–23 Paul clarifies his understanding of the role of the apostles in the church. He insists that the apostles are instruments of God and that the relationship among the apostles should be regarded as collaborative rather than competitive. He drives home this point by imagining the church in turn as a field, a building, and a temple. What counts most is the church, not the individual apostles. What is important is belonging to Christ—and thus to God—not to the human leaders who work to build up the church. And in 4:1–13 he appeals (ironically) to his own sufferings and weaknesses in the service of the gospel. Whatever wisdom Paul has comes from, and is measured by, the cross of Christ.

Sexual Morality. Among the other problems reported to Paul were two cases of sexual immorality among the Corinthian Christians. The first case (5:1–13) concerned a man who was living with "his father's wife," most likely his stepmother or a concubine belonging to his father. The woman was probably not a Christian. Such scandalous conduct was forbidden by Jewish Law (Leviticus 18:8; 20:11) and by Roman law. Paul recommended that the incestuous man be condemned and excommunicated, very likely to shock him into the recognition and acknowledgment of his sin. The second case (6:12–20) concerned Christian men who continued to visit prostitutes. Paul criticized their behavior not only as sinful on the part of those individuals but also as a sin against the community as the body of Christ. In both cases it is likely that the sinners were justifying their behavior on the grounds that "all things are lawful for me" (6:12). Paul, however, regarded their actions as contrary to the proper use of Christian freedom and offered harsh judgments on their shameful behavior.

In 1 Corinthians 7 Paul answers questions pertaining to marriage. The letter the Corinthians had sent him apparently quoted a slogan that was current in their community: "It is well for a man not to touch a woman." That line of thinking would have imposed celibacy on all Christians. Paul rejects this position and implies that the usual state for Christians is marriage (7:1–7). He recommends celibacy for widowers and widows if it is appropriate (7:8–9), forbids divorce and remarriage except in the case of a mixed marriage where the non-Christian spouse opts out (7:10–16), and recommends marriage for most unmarried persons (including widows) but praises celibacy as superior (7:25–40). Paul's basic position was that Christians should stay in the social state in which they became Christians, probably because he did not expect the present world to continue much longer ("in view of the impending crisis," 7:26).

Order at Community Gatherings. First Corinthians provides precious glimpses into the social and religious life of early Christians. In the three different cases described in chapters 11—14 Paul provides pastoral advice that is mainly concerned with insuring proper order at various Christian gatherings.

In 11:2–16 Paul assumes that women will pray and prophesy at community assemblies (11:5). His problem is with the possible blurring of the gender distinctions between men and women, either through hairstyles or the failure of women to wear veils. Perhaps there was a too literal interpretation (at least for Paul) of the baptismal slogan that in Christ "there is no longer male and female" (Galatians 3:28). In response to the Corinthians' query,

Paul insists that at the assembly for prayer and prophecy men should look like men and women should look like women.

In 11:17–34 the problem seems to have been the custom of the well-to-do members of the community gathering separately for special foods and drinks before the rest of the community arrived for the celebration of the Lord's Supper. The community as a whole depended on the generosity of whoever owned a house capable of accommodating a group of forty to fifty people. It was only natural that the owner might want to spend special time with members of his own social and economic class. However, in Paul's view, the result was that the assembly was reflecting the social and economic divisions within the community rather than the unity in Christ that the Lord's Supper should reflect. Paul's advice was for them to separate the intimate social gathering from the Eucharist.

The community gatherings described in chapters 12—14 had become the scene of a holy rivalry regarding the gifts (charisms) of the Holy Spirit. In 12:4–11 Paul insists that each Christian has a gift, that all these gifts are from the Holy Spirit, that there is a variety of gifts, and that all the gifts are meant to be used for the common good, especially in building up the body of Christ. The problem seems to have been that some Christians were exalting the exotic gift of speaking in "tongues" (glossolalia) at the expense of what they regarded as the humbler gifts. Paul's strategy was to remind the Christians that they all are members of the body of Christ, and thus they all must work together for the common good. In his list of the spiritual gifts (12:27–30) he places speaking in tongues last, and goes on in chapter 14 to exalt the gifts of prophecy and teaching on the grounds that they are intelligible to all and so can be especially useful in building up the body of Christ. Most important of all, he insists that every spiritual gift must be exercised in a spirit of love—a point made dramatically and memorably by his famous discourse on love in chapter 13.

Key Texts and Questions

Read 1 Corinthians 1:18–25. How would you describe what Paul means by wisdom and foolishness?

Read 3:1–17. What kinds of factions and divisions have you experienced in your church community? What wisdom of Paul would you try to apply to such problems?

Read 11:17–34. What problems had developed concerning the Lord's Supper in the Corinthian church? How might these problems be repeated in today's churches?

Read 13:1–13. Which qualities of love stand out for you in this passage, and why?

Read 14:26–40. Why was Paul so concerned about order at Christian gatherings?

Read 15:1–58. What connections are there between Christ's resurrection and our hope for resurrection?

Rejoice in the Lord always; again I will say, Rejoice. Let your gentleness be known to everyone. The Lord is near. Do not worry about anything, but in everything by prayer and supplication with thanksgiving let your requests be made known to God. And the peace of God, which surpasses all understanding, will guard your hearts and your minds in Christ Jesus.

—Philippians 4:4–7

The Letter to the Philippians

Philippi in northeastern Greece was named after King Philip II of Macedon, the father of Alexander the Great. After the Roman conquest of Macedonia in 168–167 B.C., it became a major stop on the highway that connected Asia Minor (present-day Turkey) and Italy. In the first century B.C. it was refounded as a Roman colony. Its religious life included the cults of various Greek and Roman deities.

According to Acts 16:11–40, Paul came to Philippi and there founded the first European Christian community. His initial success was due in large part to Lydia and other women who gathered with her for prayer. The apostle's search for a synagogue on the Sabbath and his finding only a group of women outside the city alongside the river (16:13) suggest a very small Jewish presence there. In Acts 16:14 Lydia is described as a "worshiper of God," which probably means that she was a Gentile who was very interested in Judaism but had not yet fully converted to it. The stories about Paul and Silas at Philippi bring out the Roman character of its legal system and administration (Acts 16:20–21, 35–38).

The opening of the letter to the Philippians (1:1–2) identifies Paul and Timothy as joint authors. But in 1:3 Paul moves immediately into first-person speech. The letter is directed to the Philippian Christians ("all the saints in Christ Jesus who are in Philippi"). The added phrase "with the bishops and deacons" contains the only mention of "bishops" in the undisputed Pauline letters. Their precise office or function at Philippi is not entirely clear.

The two critical problems regarding Paul's letter to the Philippians concern its literary continuity and its place and time of origin. No one disputes that Paul wrote all the material in this letter. But there are certainly rapid shifts in tone and subject matter. Some scholars (correctly, I think) regard it as a collection of materials from three letters written by Paul to the Philippians.

In chapters 1—2 Paul writes from prison, and is both encouraging and challenging to his converts. They had become his friends in the Lord, and he is quite affectionate toward them. In fact, Philippians has often been described as a "friendship letter." But in chapter 3 he makes no mention of prison, and he is confrontational and even vindictive toward rival Jewish Christian missionaries who were criticizing Paul and his gospel and trying to convince the Gentile Christians at Philippi to accept circumcision and to observe fully the Mosaic Law. In 4:10–20 Paul thanks (somewhat awkwardly) the Philippian Christians for the gift that they sent to him while he was in prison through Epaphroditus, one of Paul's coworkers.

The theory that Philippians is a collection of three pieces makes good sense of the text as it now stands. According to this theory, the earliest section would be the thank-you note (4:10–20) that Paul wrote shortly after Epaphroditus's arrival with the gift. The second and longest part (1:1–3:1a; 4:2-9, 21–23) contained Paul's pastoral advice intended to encourage and challenge his friends at Philippi. These first two parts were clearly written while Paul was in prison. Paul would have sent the main letter, perhaps along with the thank-you note, with Epaphroditus on his return to Philippi (2:25–30). The more combative section (3:1b—4:1) makes no mention of Paul's imprisonment and probably reflects the arrival of Jewish Christian missionaries at Philippi at a later time, after Paul's release. Similar problems come up in Galatians and 2 Corinthians.

There are enough references to Paul's imprisonment in Philippians to qualify it, along with Philemon, as a "prison letter." The critical question is, Where and when was Paul in prison when he wrote to the Philippians and to Philemon? Fairly late in his apostolic career, Paul was imprisoned first at Caesarea Maritima in Palestine (Acts 22:24—26:32) and then in Rome (Acts 28:16, 30–31). However, both letters envision frequent travels and communications on the part of Paul, his coworkers, and the recipients at Philippi, at much shorter distances than either Caesarea or Rome would allow. Many scholars argue that Paul had been imprisoned earlier than we learn from Acts, most likely at Ephesus (2 Corinthians 1:8–11). If so, Paul wrote his letters to the Philippians and Philemon from Ephesus between A.D. 54 and 55.

Paul had several reasons for writing to the Philippians. He wanted to reassure them about his situation in prison, to urge them to greater mutual respect and unity in the light of tensions within their community (4:2–3), to warn them against the claims of rival Jewish Christian missionaries, and to thank them for their generous gift. The most famous passage in the letter is the early Christian hymn quoted in 2:6–11.

Overview of Philippians
Opening (1:1–2)
Paul's prison letter (1:3—3:1a; 4:2–9)
Thanksgiving and prayer (1:3–11)

Overview of Philippians, cont.

Paul's present and future situation (1:12–26)

Exhortation to unity (1:27—2:5)

The hymn about Christ (2:6–11)

Further instructions (2:12–18)

Travel plans (2:19—3:1)

Paul's argument against false teachers (3:1b—4:1)

Paul's transformation (3:1b–11)

His present struggle and future hope
(3:12—4:1)

Exhortation to unity (4:2–9)

Paul's thank-you note (4:10–20)

Closing (4:21–23)

Major Themes in This Letter

Problems in Philippi. In the letter to the Philippians Paul deals with problems both inside and outside the community. The precise nature of the internal problems isn't clear. In 1:27—2:18 Paul commends greater humility, mutual respect, and union of hearts and minds. All this suggests that there were divisions within the community itself. Two women in particular—Euodia and Syntyche—are urged in 4:2 to be "of the same mind in the Lord," though we don't know their exact roles in the conflict.

The external problems confronted in 3:1b—4:1 concern the apparent arrival of Jewish Christian missionaries who wanted to impose circumcision and full observance of the Mosaic Law on the Gentile Christians at Philippi. Paul dismisses them vehemently as "dogs . . . evil workers . . . those who mutilate the flesh" (3:2). It's obvious that Paul is referring to their promotion of circumcision for Gentile Christians. He concludes by claiming that they are "enemies of the cross of Christ" (3:18), since they are in effect calling into question that Jesus' death and resurrection were sufficient to bring about right relationship with God (justification). Paul's charge in 3:19 that "their god is the belly" alludes disparagingly to the Jewish food laws, and his observation that "their glory is in their shame" seems to be yet another sarcastic reference to circumcision. Keep in mind that these rival missionaries were Paul's fellow Jewish Christians.

The Christ-Hymn. The theological highlight of Paul's letter to the Philippians is the early Christian hymn about the humiliation and exaltation of Christ the Servant of God that is quoted in 2:6–11. It appears that Paul is quoting material already in existence; it doesn't fit gracefully into the text around it, and, compared to the rest of the letter, the language of this short passage is peculiar—"the form of God . . . equality with God . . . something to be exploited," etc. The original language seems to have been Aramaic, since the present Greek text can be translated back into Aramaic without great difficulty. Since Paul wrote to the Philippians in the early to mid-50s of the first century, this hymn offers an important glimpse into very early Christian beliefs about Jesus.

The first stanza of the hymn (2:6–8) describes Christ as equal to God, his self-emptying in becoming human, and his obedience to his Father shown in his suffering a shameful death on the cross. The second stanza (2:9–11) celebrates his resurrection and exaltation of Christ as Lord (*kyrios* in Greek) and the homage paid to him by all creation.

Paul introduced this hymn into his letter to the Philippians to provide a Christ-centered foundation for his exhortation that Christians develop greater humility and mutual respect within their community. For Paul, the key phrase was "he humbled himself" (2:8), since in the letter he uses the hymn to encourage an attitude of humbly regarding "others as better than yourselves" (2:3).

Paul's Transformation. The letter to the Philippians offers a glimpse into Paul's complex character. As we have seen, when dealing with what he regarded as a perversion of the gospel in 3:1b—4:1, Paul could be combative and even nasty. In thanking the Philippians for their gift in 4:10–20, he is at best awkward. Scholars have speculated about what this gift was—from a supply of good food to enough money to buy his way out of jail. At the start of the note Paul is a bit insulting ("at last you have revived your concern for me") and condescending ("I have learned to be content with whatever I have"). Eventually he comes around to a gracious acknowledgement of the gift and a prayer on behalf of those who sent it.

However, in chapters 1 and 2 the personal transformation that Paul underwent in light of his experience of the risen Christ shines through. In 1:12–26 Paul seeks to reassure the Philippians about his imprisonment. Rather than complaining about his sufferings, he expresses the positive conviction that his imprisonment has served to advance the spread of the gospel among his captors ("the whole imperial guard") and to challenge other Christian preachers (even his rivals) to proclaim the gospel more boldly. As he faces the possibility that he might be executed, Paul exhibits a remarkable indifference: "For to me, living is Christ and dying is gain" (1:21). If he lives, he will continue to spread the gospel. If he dies, he will be more fully with Christ. At the root of this optimistic attitude is the transformation that he had experienced through "the surpassing value of knowing Christ Jesus my Lord" (3:8). That experience of right relationship with God led Paul to look upon his otherwise superb credentials as a Jew to be "loss" and even "rubbish." Paul's ideal in life was to be more and more like Christ: "I want to know Christ and the power of his resurrection and the sharing of his sufferings by becoming like him in his death, if somehow I may attain the resurrection from the dead" (3:10–11).

Key Texts and Questions

Read Philippians 1:12–26. What helped Paul cope with his imprisonment?

Read 2:5–11. In light of the hymn preserved in Philippians 2:6–11, what did early Christians believe about Jesus?

Read 3:1–11. What was Paul's attitude toward his former Jewish practices?

I am appealing to you for my child, Onesimus, whose father I have become during my imprisonment. Formerly he was useless to you, but now he is indeed useful both to you and to me. I am sending him, that, is, my own heart, back to you. I wanted to keep him with me, so that he might be of service to me in your place during my imprisonment for the gospel; but I preferred to do nothing without your consent, in order that your good deed might be voluntary and not something forced. Perhaps this is the reason he was separated from you for a while, so that you might have him back forever, no longer as a slave but more than a slave, a beloved brother—especially to me but how much more to you, both in the flesh and in the Lord.

—Philemon 10–16

The Letter to Philemon

The letter to Philemon is the shortest of the four Pauline letters addressed to individuals, and so it comes last in the thirteen epistles attributed to Paul. There is no doubt about its direct Pauline authorship. However, it is not simply a private communication. It was sent from Paul and Timothy to Philemon, Apphia, and Archippus, as well as to "the church in your house."

Paul is in prison, most likely at Ephesus. Philemon was one of Paul's converts and Apphia most likely Philemon's wife. They seem to have lived in Colossae, in western Asia Minor. There Philemon had made available his house for meetings of the local Christian community. Archippus ("our fellow soldier") was associated in some way with Paul's network or team of missionaries (Colossians 4:17). The letter was written about the same time as Philippians—that is, around A.D. 54–55. In it Paul requests that Philemon take Onesimus back into his household.

Who was Onesimus? The traditional interpretation (at least since John Chrysostom) views him as a slave belonging to Philemon. Onesimus probably knew Paul from Paul's dealings with his master. Perhaps because of some financial misdealing ("if he has wronged you in any way, or owes you anything," v. 18), Onesimus left or fled Philemon's household. Whether he was legally a "fugitive" slave (for whom penalties under Roman law were severe) is not clear. According to this scenario, Onesimus sought out Paul, became a Christian, and was assisting Paul in prison. Now Paul was asking Philemon to take Onesimus back without penalty "no longer as a slave but more than a slave, a beloved brother" (v. 16).

Another line of interpretation views Onesimus as Philemon's brother, who had committed some financial misdealing but later became a Christian under Paul's guidance. In this scenario Paul is asking Philemon to reinstate his blood brother Onesimus in his household as "a beloved brother" without recrimination. Most interpreters today follow the "runaway slave" interpretation. Scholars are still debating about whether or not Paul expected Philemon to free Onesimus from slavery.

Overview of Philemon
Opening (1–3)
Thanksgiving: Faith and love (4–7)
Paul's request (8–21)
Appeal to Philemon (8–12)
Onesimus's return (13–16)
Paul's bargain (17–21)
Closing (22–25)

Major Themes in This Letter

Paul's Powers of Persuasion. The letter to Philemon is a rhetorical tour-de-force in which Paul uses various means to persuade Philemon to do what he regarded as the right thing. At the outset he identifies himself as "a prisoner of Christ Jesus" and reminds Philemon several times of his own suffering for the gospel (vv. 9, 10, 13, 23). In the thanksgiving he emphasizes that faith should manifest itself in love, in a sense warming up for the primary request in this letter. Instead of commanding Philemon, he appeals to him on the basis of love. He even uses a slight play on words, claiming that Onesimus—a name meaning something like "useful"—who was formerly useless to Philemon has become useful to Paul and can now be useful to Philemon. He reminds Philemon of the spiritual debt that he owes to Paul for bringing him to Christian faith and tells him to charge it to Paul's account. He concludes by expressing confidence that Philemon will comply with this request, and promises to visit him when he gets out of jail (when he will verify Philemon's compliance). And recall that the letter is intended to be read before "the church in your house." This is a remarkable example of rhetorical persuasion, if not manipulation!

The Issue of Slavery. Did Paul expect Philemon to free Onesimus from slavery? We might come to this conclusion on the basis of Paul's request that Philemon receive Onesimus "no longer as a slave but more than a slave" (v. 16). There is mention of an Onesimus in Colossians 4:9, and someone by that name became bishop of Ephesus some sixty years later. However, it is unlikely that Paul went so far in his advocacy for Onesimus. The Roman Empire was a slave economy. To ask Philemon to free Onesimus would have entailed a financial sacrifice on his part and would probably have won him the hostility of other slaveholders in his social class.

Not only that, but Paul believed that "this world" was passing away, and so elsewhere (1 Corinthians 7:21–24) he urges slaves who became Christians to remain in their condition. In

Galatians 3:28 Paul quotes an early Christian baptismal formula according to which "there is no longer slave or free . . . in Christ Jesus." Yet Paul and other early Christians most likely understood their new identity in Christ as transcending rather than abolishing differences in ethnicity ("no longer Jew or Greek"), social status ("no longer slave or free"), and gender ("no longer male and female").

The House Church. Paul's mention of "the church in your house" in the salutation (v. 2) alludes to an important aspect of early Christian life. The first Christians did not build churches or temples. Rather, they came together in private homes like those of Philemon and of Aquila and Prisca (1 Corinthians 16:19; Romans 16:5). The houses of such relatively well-to-do Christians might accommodate anywhere from twenty to fifty persons. The house's owner and his wife would naturally have been prominent at these gatherings, and probably they exercised some measure of control and authority over the group. Paul's description of the tensions that arose in such a setting at Corinth (1 Corinthians 11:17–34) shows that this arrangement could generate its own set of problems. Still, the house church did allow for a certain level of intimacy and solidarity that was lost when larger facilities became available.

Key Texts and Questions

Read Philemon 1:8–16. How does Paul try to persuade Philemon to accept Onesimus back as his "beloved brother"? What message does this letter give about slavery in antiquity and about early Christian social life?

To keep me from being too elated, a thorn was given me in the flesh, a messenger of Satan to torment me, to keep me from being too elated. Three times I appealed to the Lord about this, that it would leave me, but he said to me, "My grace is sufficient for you, for power is made perfect in weakness. So, I will boast all the more gladly of my weaknesses, so that the power of Christ may dwell in me. Therefore I am content with weaknesses, insults, hardships, persecutions, and calamities for the sake of Christ; for whenever I am weak, then I am strong.

—2 Corinthians 12:7–10

The Second Letter to the Corinthians

The letter known as 2 Corinthians is the third longest among the Pauline letters. It comes from Paul and Timothy, and is addressed to "the church of God that is in Corinth, including all the saints throughout Achaia" (1:1–2). It must have been written after 1 Corinthians, and it is usually dated to sometime in the fall of A.D. 54 or 55. It is quite different in tone and purpose from 1 Corinthians. Paul appears to have been in Macedonia at the time of its writing. His plan to revisit Corinth (1 Corinthians 16:5) seems not to have been carried out (2 Corinthians 1:16). Timothy, whom he had sent to Corinth (1 Corinthians 4:17; 16:10), had returned to Paul in Macedonia (2 Corinthians 1:1).

In the meantime Paul's person and ministry had been attacked both from within the Corinthian community and from outside, most likely by Jewish Christian missionaries such as those in Galatia and Philippi who raised questions about Paul's gospel and his practice of not insisting that Gentile Christians undergo circumcision and observe the Mosaic Law. In 2:4 (see also 2:9) Paul refers to a letter that he wrote to the Corinthians "out of much distress and anguish of heart and with many tears." Much of 2 Corinthians has to do with Paul defending himself and his apostleship.

The present text of 2 Corinthians contains many changes in tone and other loose ends. Many scholars today defend its literary unity, and argue that the letter we now have is pretty much the way Paul wrote it. They attribute the rough spots and changes in tone to the many different subjects treated in the letter and the possibility that Paul wrote it over a period of time rather than at

one sitting. However, other scholars regard 2 Corinthians as a collection of smaller pieces, much like the letter to the Philippians.
There is little doubt that all the parts (except perhaps 6:14—7:1)
were composed by Paul. But it seems likely that what we now have
in 2 Corinthians is a compilation of shorter communications sent
over time by Paul to the Corinthians, which have now been gathered into one very large "letter."

Those who view 2 Corinthians as a collection argue that the
material in 1:1—2:13 flows nicely into 7:5–16 in both content and
tone, and that those two sections may once have constituted a separate letter. The intervening material in 2:14—6:13 about the ministry is very rich historically and theologically but seems to interrupt
the more pragmatic first letter. The warning against unbelievers in
6:14—7:1 is quite dualistic (righteousness vs. lawlessness, light vs.
darkness, Christ vs. Beliar, believer vs. unbeliever) and has many
parallels with texts found among the Dead Sea Scrolls. Those who
defend its Pauline origin suggest that it may have been the letter
from Paul mentioned in 1 Corinthians 5:9. The section devoted to
the collection for the Christian community in Jerusalem (chapters
8—9) contains many repetitions, and may well have once been
two shorter letters. The combative and sarcastic tone of Paul's self-
defense in chapters 10—13 does not fit well with the apparent reso-
lution between Paul and the Corinthians reached in 7:5–16. Some
scholars suggest that this section may once have been the "tearful
letter" mentioned in 2:4, 9.

One attempt made by Günther Bornkamm and Dieter
Georgi to arrange all these smaller communications in their
possible original chronological order goes like this: Letter A =

2:14—7:4 (with 6:14—7:1 understood as a later interpolation);
Letter B = 10:1—13:10; Letter C = 1:1—2:13 + 7:5–16; Letter D
= 8:1–24; and Letter E = 9:1–15. We don't know who arranged
the material in its present form and why he did so in exactly
this way. Whether we choose to read 2 Corinthians as one long
and meandering letter or as a collection of several short letters,
it remains one of the most personal and revealing letters connected with Paul. At the same time, it contains rich insights on
a variety of topics.

Overview of 2 Corinthians
Opening (1:1–2)
Benediction (1:3–11)
Changes in travel plans (1:12—2:13)
The apostolic ministry (2:14—7:16)
　　Triumphal procession (2:14–17)
　　Old and new covenants (3:1–18)
　　Treasures in earthen vessels (4:1–15)
　　Life and death (4:16—5:10)
　　Ministry of reconciliation (5:11—6:13)
　　Warnings against unbelievers (6:14—7:1)
　　Good news from Titus (7:2–16)
The collection (8:1—9:15)
　　Reasons for generosity (8:1–15)
　　Commendation of Titus (8:16–24)
　　More reasons for generosity (9:1–15)
Paul's defense of his apostleship (10:1—13:10)
　　Responses to criticisms (10:1–18)

> **Overview of 2 Corinthians,** cont.
> Critique of the false apostles (11:1–15)
> The fool's speech (11:16—12:13)
> Plans for a third visit (12:14—13:10)
> Closing (13:11–13)

Major Themes in This Letter

Old and New Covenants. As he did in Philippians 3 and Galatians, Paul is writing mainly to Gentile Christians and trying to dissuade them from following the rival Jewish Christian missionaries. In order to drive home the point that followers of Jesus are not obligated to keep Jewish laws, Paul points out a series of sharp contrasts between the old covenant (inaugurated with Moses on Sinai) and the new covenant (inaugurated by Jesus).

For instance, Paul contends that

the old covenant is based on the letter, but the new
    covenant is based on the Spirit of the living God;
the old covenant brings death, but the new
    covenant brings life;
the old covenant brings condemnation, but the new
    covenant brings righteousness;
glory surrounds the giving of the old covenant,
    but even more splendor accompanies the new
    covenant;

> the old covenant is read through a veil, but Christ
> has set aside the veil and allows us to see the
> glory of God with unveiled faces.

The conclusion of Paul's contrasts appears in 3:17: "Now the Lord is the Spirit, and where the Spirit of the Lord is, there is freedom."

The Collection. Paul regarded the collection for the church at Jerusalem not only as a charitable action but also as a symbol of the spiritual unity existing between Gentiles and Jews in the church. He had already instructed the Corinthians to put aside a certain amount every week so that when he came to Corinth, there would be a substantial amount already amassed (1 Corinthians 16:1–4). Paul's plan was to bring the proceeds of the collections taken up in his Gentile Christian churches to the Jewish "mother church" in Jerusalem as a sign of the spiritual debt that Gentile Christians owed to Jewish Christians.

Second Corinthians 8—9 is often described as the first Christian fundraising letter. Given the repetitions in the two chapters, it is possible that each chapter was once a separate fundraising letter. In chapter 8 Paul praises the Macedonian churches for their generosity, and hopes that the Corinthians will match it. Then he appeals in turn to the generosity exemplified by Christ, to their sense of justice and fairness, and to Scripture (Exodus 16:18). He concludes by promising to send his esteemed coworker Titus to receive the proceeds, and by hoping to be able to boast over their contribution as "the proof of your love" (8:24).

In chapter 9 Paul first indulges in what has been described as "moral blackmail" by pleading that anything less than the Corinthians' very generous contribution will make him look bad for having boasted so much about them. Then he appeals to a proverb ("one who sows sparingly will also reap sparingly . . ."), to the character of God ("God loves a cheerful giver"), and to Scripture again (Psalm 112:9). He concludes by assuring the Corinthians that God will surely bless them for their great generosity and by suggesting that their gifts are ways of giving thanks to God for God's many gifts to them.

The Sufferings of the Apostle. Many parts of 2 Corinthians indicate that Paul had been severely criticized and attacked. Paul responded to these attacks by reminding the Corinthians about the many sufferings he had endured for the sake of the gospel. He also pointed to his personal weaknesses and sufferings as proofs that his ministry was genuine and initiated by God.

In 6:3–10 Paul lists the physical and emotional hardships that he had endured for the gospel and dismisses them as of no real account when compared to the grace of carrying out his mission as an apostle. In 10:10, we learn that his opponents had been saying, "His letters are weighty and strong, but his bodily presence is weak and his speech contemptible." In his "fool's speech" (11:1—12:13) Paul answers those critics (whom he sarcastically calls "super-apostles") by boasting not of his strengths but rather of his weaknesses. Though he lists once more his exemplary credentials as a Jew in 11:21–22, he goes on to offer a catalogue of his sufferings and degradations in the service of the ministry.

Paul mentions his visionary mystical experiences in a rather vague way in 12:1–4, but he focuses more on his "thorn in the flesh" that has kept him humble throughout all his spiritual and apostolic achievements. The precise nature of this thorn is not known. Guesses have ranged from a speech impediment to epilepsy, and practically everything else. But the point of Paul's strategy in defending his apostleship becomes clear when he describes his prayer that the thorn might be removed, and how he received as an answer from God, "My grace is sufficient for you, for power is made perfect in weakness" (12:9).

Key Texts and Questions

Read 2 Corinthians 3:6–18. How are the old and new covenants related?

Read 5:1–10. How does Paul encourage the reader to think about the human body, and about death?

Read 5:14–21. What does reconciliation mean in regard to Christ and the world?

Read 6:3–10. How did Paul regard his sufferings as an apostle?

Therefore, since we are justified by faith, we have peace with God through our Lord Jesus Christ, through whom we have obtained access to this grace in which we stand; and we boast in our hope of sharing the glory of God. And not only that, but we also boast in our sufferings, knowing that suffering produces endurance, and endurance produces character, and character produces hope, and hope does not disappoint us, because God's love has been poured into our hearts through the Holy Spirit that has been given to us.

—Romans 5:1–5

The Letter to the Romans

Paul did not found the church at Rome. Christianity took root very early in the large Jewish community at Rome, and by the 40s of the first century A.D. it had become a lively movement. When Jews and Jewish Christians were expelled from Rome under the emperor Claudius in A.D. 49 (Acts 18:2)—most likely in a dispute about "Chrestos" (probably Christ)—the Gentile Christians at Rome took control of the church there. When Jews and Jewish Christians were allowed to return to Rome in A.D. 54, the Jewish Christians naturally expected to resume their positions of prominence and leadership. The Gentile Christians apparently did not agree, and so there were tensions between the two groups.

Paul had not yet visited the church at Rome. He wrote his letter to the Romans in A.D. 56 or 57 from Corinth (16:21–23). He apparently knew many Christians who were now in Rome (16:1–16), and he hoped to spend time in Rome before moving on to begin a new mission in Spain (15:24, 28). Before that, however, he planned to bring the proceeds of the collection he had taken up in various Gentile Christian communities he had founded in Asia Minor and Greece (15:25). It is likely that Phoebe, "a deacon of the church at Cenchreae" (16:1), the port city of Corinth, took Paul's letter to Rome.

More than any other letter of Paul, Romans gives the impression of being a formal essay on the topic of the gospel. By "the gospel" Paul meant the good news of Jesus Christ, especially with reference to his death and resurrection, and their consequences for believers. The outline that follows shows how every part of the letter deals with some aspect of the gospel. Romans stands out as the longest and most comprehensive statement of Paul's theology in the New Testament.

Nevertheless, the letter to the Romans is still the work of Paul the pastor. He had several purposes in writing this letter to the Romans. In preparation for his planned visit he wanted to introduce himself to the Roman Christians and present to them a summary of the gospel that he hoped to proclaim in Spain. Perhaps he was responding to suspicions and criticisms that had been raised about his teaching and practice. At Jerusalem Paul probably expected not only to present the proceeds of the collection but also to answer questions from the local church leaders there. In effect, he was preparing a more systematic—and less emotional—defense of his Law-free gospel for non-Jews than he had provided to the Galatians. It also seems that, in light of his words about the equality and unity that Jesus' death and resurrection had brought about between Jews and Gentiles, Paul hoped to help the Roman Christians to deal more effectively with the conflicts in their own faith community (see 14:1—15:13).

There is no doubt that Paul wrote the letter to the Romans, though he seems to have employed the services of a scribe named Tertius (16:22). The final warning (16:17–20) and the doxology (16:25–27) may well have been added later by someone else to the list of greetings to Christians at Rome (16:1–16) from those with Paul at Corinth (16:21–23). The list of those greeted includes a large number of women, several of whom are called Paul's coworkers, as well as a deacon (Phoebe) and an apostle (Junia).

Overview of Romans

The gospel defined (1:1–17)
   Opening greeting (1:1–7)
   Thanksgiving and wish (1:8–15)
   The gospel as the power of God (1:16–17)
The need for the gospel (1:18—3:20)
   Gentiles needed the gospel (1:18–32)
   Jews needed the gospel (2:1–29)
      Despite their moral superiority (2:1–11)
      Despite possessing the Torah (2:12–24)
      Despite circumcision (2:25–29)
   Objections and answers (3:1–8)
   The universal dominion of sin (3:9–20)
The gospel and faith (3:21—4:25)
   God's righteousness and faith (3:21–26)
   No grounds for boasting (3:27–31)
   Abraham was justified (4:1–17)
      By faith (4:1–8)
      Before circumcision (4:9–12)
      Before the Law (4:13–17)
   Abraham as the example of faith (4:18–25)
The gospel and freedom (5:1—7:25)
   What God has done in Christ (5:1–11)
   Adam and Christ (5:12–21)
   Freedom from the power of sin and death
      (6:1–11)
   Freed for obedience to God (6:12–23)
   Freed from the Law (7:1–6)
   Sin and the Law (7:7–11)

Overview of Romans, cont.

Life under sin and the Law (7:12–25)

The gospel and life in the Spirit (8:1–39)

Life in the Spirit (8:1–11)

Children of God (8:12–17)

Waiting in hope (8:18–25)

The Spirit and prayer (8:26–27)

God is for us (8:28–39)

The gospel and God's plan (9:1—11:36)

Paul's lament and Israel's privileges (9:1–5)

The surprising way of God (9:6–13)

God's sovereign freedom and justice
(9:14–24)

The present state of God's people and
Scripture (9:25–29)

Israel's mistake (9:30–10:4)

Biblical confirmation (10:5–13)

Accepting and rejecting the gospel (10:14–21)

A remnant within Israel (11:1–10)

Jews and Gentiles (11:11–16)

The olive tree (11:17–24)

The mystery of salvation (11:25–32)

Celebratory conclusion (11:33–36)

The gospel and Christian life (12:1—13:14)

The body of Christ and the gifts of the Spirit
(12:1–8)

Love toward others (12:9–21)

Christian life in the Roman Empire (13:1–7)

Overview of Romans, cont.
The love command and the day of the Lord
(13:8–14)
The gospel and community conflict (14:1—15:13)
Avoid condemning others (14:1–12)
Respect for the conscience of others
(14:13–23)
The example of Christ (15:1–6)
Christ as the principle of unity (15:7–13)
The promotion of the gospel (15:14—16:27)
Apostle to the Gentiles (15:14–21)
Travel plans (15:22–33)
Final greetings (16:1–16)
Warning (16:17–20)
More greetings (16:21–23)
Doxology (16:25–27)

Major Themes in This Letter

The Gospel. The good news or "gospel" about Jesus' life, death, and resurrection—and its implications for believers—is the theme that runs through the entire letter to the Romans. In the letter's opening Paul quotes an early Christian profession of faith (1:3–4) that summarizes some of the gospel's content. In 1:16–17 Paul describes the gospel as "the power of God for salvation to everyone who has faith, to the Jew first and also to the Greek." The theological focus of Romans is the significance of Jesus' death and resurrection for the salvation of human-kind. Paul insists that faith is where the story of our salvation is played out ("through faith for faith," 1:17). We become part of this story through faith in both its subjective (trust) and objective (beliefs) dimensions.

In 2:1—3:20 Paul argues that all people—both Gentiles and Jews—needed the revelation of God's righteousness or justice through Christ. By refusing to recognize the hand of God in creation and left to their own devices, the Gentiles fell into a downward spiral of ignorance and vice. Even with the divine guidance supplied by the Torah, the Jews failed to observe God's Law and they too found themselves condemned as sinners before God. Paul's grim conclusion is that before and apart from Christ "all have sinned and fall short of the glory of God" (3:23).

To remedy the sorry state of humankind, God took the initiative through the redemptive death of Jesus and his resurrection from the dead. He became the "sacrifice of atonement" (3:25), with the result that all humans—Jews and Gentiles alike—can participate in the new relationship with God now made possible through Jesus. We can do so by following the example of Abraham (4:1–25), the "ancestor of all who believe" (4:11). This is the gospel, the good news of Jesus Christ.

Our Salvation through Christ. In his letter to the Romans (and in his other letters), Paul pays relatively little attention to teachings, miracles, and other activities of the earthly Jesus. Instead, he focuses almost entirely on Jesus' death and resurrection. And even there he shows little interest in the precise details of Jesus' passion, death, and resurrection. In Romans Paul's concern is not so much Christology as it is the saving significance of Jesus, or the effects of his death and resurrection.

One of the most prominent themes in Paul's writings (and in subsequent Christian theology) is justification. This term has legal roots. In Romans Paul uses it to refer to the acquittal of humans before the judgment seat of God. While in Jewish religious writings of that time the term *justification* was reserved for the last judgment, Paul was convinced that justification had already occurred through Jesus' death and resurrection. That means that the new relationship with God hoped for in the last judgment is already available through Christ in the present for persons of faith.

There are other aspects of this new relationship with God that are mentioned in Paul's letters. For example, Paul uses the term "salvation" to describe the divinely initiated rescue from moral and physical evil in the present and life in the future kingdom of God. Other terms used in describing what God has done for us in Christ include *redemption, reconciliation, sanctification,* and *glorification.*

All these terms are ways of describing our liberation from our slavery to sin, death, and the Law, and of being freed for life in the Holy Spirit. This process is described in great detail in Romans 5—8. In Paul's reconstruction of God's saving action, humankind from Adam onward found itself enslaved through its own sinfulness. Death came into the world through Adam's sin. When the Law was given to Moses on Sinai, even the Law began to function as a stimulus to sin, which in turn led to death. The primary effect of Jesus' death and resurrection was to make possible a new beginning. That new beginning is described in Romans 8 as life in the Spirit—that is, the possibility of the human person being led by, and responding to, the Holy Spirit. Some of the practical implications are spelled out in the "ethical section" in Romans 12—15.

The Mystery of Israel. Paul was thoroughly convinced that what God had done in Christ has significance for all peoples, not simply Israel. Thus he took his call to be the apostle to the Gentiles with great seriousness. However, it pained him (9:1–5) that not all his fellow Jews saw things as he did. And so in a complicated and sometimes meandering meditation in Romans 9—11, Paul tried to understand and explain the divine plan for Jews and Gentiles in salvation history.

In Paul's drama of salvation history there are three major entities: Jewish Christians like Paul, Gentile Christians, and non-Christian Jews. Jewish Christians served as the link between Israel as the historic people of God and the Christian movement (which Paul regarded as the fullness of Judaism). Jewish Christians are the "remnant" mentioned in various biblical texts. Paul could not imagine the church without an organic connection to historic Israel as the people of God.

Paul was convinced that what God had done in Christ had immense significance even for non-Jews. Through his missionary activities, Paul sought to bring as many Gentiles as possible into the people of God in Christ. But what about those Jews who did not accept the gospel? They were a puzzle to Paul, and in 9:1–5 he agonized over their unwillingness to accept the gospel. However, in a kind of "eureka" moment described in Romans 11, Paul thought that he had finally figured out God's strategy in salvation history. The success of the Gentile mission was intended to shake those Jews out of their complacency and make them jealous (11:11–12) of what Gentiles were experiencing through Christ—freedom from sin, death, and the Law, and freedom for life in the Spirit.

Paul developed his insight first with an analogy about the olive tree in 11:17–24. The roots of the olive tree are Jewish Christians like himself. The Gentile Christians are branches from a wild olive shoot that have been grafted onto the olive tree that represents the people of God. The non-Christian Jews are branches that have been broken off from the olive tree "because of their unbelief" (11:20). But they are not totally lost. Indeed, if God could graft branches from the wild olive shoot onto the tree, how much more easily can God graft the natural branches back onto the olive tree!

In 11:25b–26a Paul summarizes his entire argument: "a hardening has come upon part of Israel, until the full number of Gentiles has come in. And so all Israel will be saved." He explains the present unbelief of part of Israel in terms of a "hardening," thus echoing the language of Isaiah 6:9–11. He supposes that there is a fixed number or quota of Gentiles who will become part of God's people in Christ. And then he expects that "all Israel will be saved." Unfortunately Paul left unanswered some important questions about Israel's salvation. Does "all Israel" include each and every Jew, or is it a collective expression? When will all Israel's salvation occur—at the end of human history (the eschaton), or throughout history? And how will it occur—through God's action at the end of human history, or through missionary activity?

Key Texts and Questions

Read Romans 3:21–26. Why did all people—Jews and Gentiles—need the gospel?

Read 4:18–25. Why was Abraham considered righteous? And what does that have to do with our faith today?

Read 7:14–25. How do you relate to what Paul said about his own interior conflict?

Read 8:28–39. On what does Paul place his hope and confidence about our future as God's people?

Read 12:1–8. What does it mean for you to be part of the body of Christ?

3

What Do We Learn from Later Pauline Letters?

It has become customary among biblical scholars to distinguish between the undisputed or authentic letters of Paul and the secondary or *Deuteropauline* letters. The *Deuteropaulines* include:

2 Thessalonians
Colossians
Ephesians
1 and 2 Timothy
Titus

Some scholars simply deny the distinction in one or all of the cases, and place these letters in a later period of Paul's career. Of course, in either theory, all these letters are considered Christian Scripture; had this not been the case, they would never have been included in the canon of Scripture we know as the Bible.

Letters Identified as "Deuteropauline"

Second Thessalonians seems to be an imitation and updating of 1 Thessalonians. Although many scholars regard Colossians as written directly by Paul, there are also good arguments for viewing it as Deuteropauline. Ephesians appears to be a revised and expanded version of Colossians. 1 Timothy and Titus are mainly concerned with church order and the place of Christians in Greco-Roman society, while 2 Timothy reads like a testament or farewell letter from Paul to his longtime coworker Timothy. All three of these "pastoral" epistles seem to reflect a period in church history sometime after Paul's death.

Here are some of the common reasons for classifying these letters as Deuteropauline.

> Their language and style are different from the letters we feel certain were written by Paul directly.
> They deal with issues that would have become more prominent in Christian communities during the period after Paul's death—such as local church offices and structures, and the delay in Christ's second coming.
> The theology contains different emphases from Paul's other letters.

The Deuteropauline letters were not produced by a single person. Rather, they represent the work of several different persons or groups. All of these writers were clearly admirers of Paul, perhaps even once coworkers with Paul, and all were committed to carrying on the heritage of his teaching and adapting it to new circumstances. Whether the first recipients of these letters knew that they were not written directly by Paul is not clear. At any rate, they would have received them (and we should too) as authentic developments of the Pauline tradition that spoke to and illumined the theological and practical problems facing their Christian communities in the late first century.

As to the coming of our Lord Jesus Christ and our being gathered together to him, we beg you, brothers and sisters, not to be quickly shaken in mind or alarmed, either by spirit or by word or by letter, as though from us, to the effect that the day of the Lord is already here. Let no one deceive you in any way; for that day will not come unless the rebellion comes first and the lawless one is revealed, the one destined for destruction.

—2 Thessalonians 2:1–3

The Second Letter to the Thessalonians

The letter known as 2 Thessalonians opens (1:1–2) in almost the same way as 1 Thessalonians does. The letter indicates Paul, Silvanus, and Timothy as joint authors. However, there is much more "we" language in the main text, and so the pretense of joint authorship is carried out more consistently than in other Pauline letters. It is addressed to "the church of the Thessalonians in God our Father and the Lord Jesus Christ." The "grace and peace" greeting (1:2) is expanded by yet another mention of "God our Father and the Lord Jesus Christ" (Romans 1:7).

If this is a genuine letter of Paul's, then it would have been written (as 1 Thessalonians was) from Corinth in A.D. 50 or 51, as a follow-up to what seems to have been the earlier letter. Its function would have been to correct and clear up certain misunderstandings perhaps connected with statements in the first letter. This scenario would explain why there are so many similarities between the two letters: the same opening, the unusual presence of two thanksgivings, the concentration on end-time matters, the many references to the first letter, and so on.

However, a good case can also be made for reading 2 Thessalonians as a later imitation of 1 Thessalonians. This interpretation would just as easily explain the similarities in language and content between the two letters. The very strong affirmation of Paul's authorship at the end ("I, Paul, write this greeting with my own hand," 3:17) can be viewed either as hard historical evidence that Paul wrote it or as a convention of imitation used at that time.

There are some notable differences between the two letters. While the vocabulary is much the same, the style has been described as "wooden" and the tone is much less affectionate and personal in comparison with 1 Thessalonians. Also, there are references to other Pauline letters already in circulation (2:2; 3:17), which may suggest greater temporal distance from 1 Thessalonians.

Both letters concern end-time events and eschatological hopes, with particular attention given to the second coming of Christ. But whereas in 1 Thessalonians 4:13–18 this seems imminent during Paul's lifetime, 2 Thessalonians 2:1–12 pushes it off into the future and explains what figures must arise and what events must take place before the second coming can happen. The basic thesis of 2 Thessalonians appears in 2:2, where the author begs his audience "not to be quickly shaken in mind or alarmed, either by spirit or by word or by letter, as though from us, to the effect that the day of the Lord is already here." This letter seeks to cool off speculations about end-times and to urge its recipients to go on with their everyday life and work.

If the case for 2 Thessalonians as Deuteropauline is persuasive, then we know little or nothing about the precise historical circumstances in which it was composed. The author was clearly an admirer of Paul, and imitation is the sincerest form of flattery. Perhaps he was even one of Paul's younger coworkers, writing sometime after Paul's death. If Ephesus became a center for Paul's teaching after Paul's death, then we can imagine a connection there.

Besides being an exercise in imitating the language and thought of Paul the apostle, 2 Thessalonians may well have been written to suggest how Paul, had he lived longer, would have explained the apparent delay of the second coming of Christ. Thus the letter stands in continuity with Paul and at the same time adapts and adjusts Paul's thought to the new realities of later history. It may have been composed around A.D. 80 or 90, perhaps even around the time of the book of Revelation. Whether it was written for or to a specific congregation is not at all certain. It could have been intended as simply a theological exercise for a student of Paul—or it could have been a general letter to several congregations.

Overview of 2 Thessalonians
Opening (1:1–2)
Thanksgiving (1:3–12)
    First thanksgiving (1:3–4)
    The coming judgment (1:5–10)
    Prayer (1:11–12)
Instructions (2:1–14)
    Signs preceding the second coming (2:1–12)
    Second thanksgiving (2:13–14)
Exhortations (2:15—3:15)
    General exhortations and prayers (2:15—3:5)
    Idleness and disobedience (3:6–15)
Final blessing and greeting (3:16–18)

Major Themes in This Letter

The Last Judgment. In 1:5–10, the author offers a vivid picture of the last judgment, at which the risen Christ will preside and serve as the judge. The assumption is that his second coming is one event in a sequence of events that will include the general resurrection of the dead, the last judgment, and rewards for the righteous and punishments for the wicked. A similar scene appears in the famous "sheep and goats" judgment passage in Matthew 25:31–46.

In 1 Thessalonians 4:13–18, Paul focused on Christ's coming and judgment as marking the vindication of the righteous; the author of 2 Thessalonians emphasizes more the lordship of Jesus made manifest in taking vengeance on the wicked, to the point of their "eternal destruction, separated from the presence of the Lord and from the glory of his might" (1:9). The last judgment thus becomes the solution to the problem of the innocent suffering undergone by the Christian readers during their lives on earth.

One enduring problem connected with belief in God is the challenge of fitting together three ideas: God is all-powerful; God is just; and innocent people suffer. One solution to this problem rests upon belief in life after death and a final judgment that will right all wrongs. Then God's omnipotence and justice will be fully visible—and the righteous will be rewarded and the wicked will be punished. Rooted in Jewish beliefs of the time, this approach was taken over by early Christians, who then gave pride of place to the risen Christ as the ultimate judge and the one who would hand out rewards and punishments.

The Delay of Christ's Second Coming. In 1 Thessalonians Paul suggests that he expects to be alive when Christ returns: "we who are alive, who are left until the coming of the Lord, will by no means precede those who have died" (4:15). Meanwhile, he urges the Thessalonians to go about their everyday lives in a spirit of hope and constant vigilance on the grounds that "the day of the Lord will come like a thief in the night" (5:2; see also 5:4), indicating that there will be little or no warning before the day of Christ's return and the last judgment. The message: Always be prepared!

The author of 2 Thessalonians takes a different approach. Of course, Paul might have changed his mind. But the hypothesis of a later author seems more likely. In 2:3–10 this author introduces a series of characters and events that must precede Christ's return. Recall that his major purpose in writing was to refute the claim that "the day of the Lord is already here" (2:2). With still another apocalyptic scenario, he insists that "the rebellion" and the revelation of "the lawless one" must come first. Even then the lawless one will be restrained. And when "the one who now restrains" will be removed, then the lawless one will be fully revealed, only to be destroyed by "the Lord Jesus" at his coming (2:8).

Over the centuries theologians and biblical scholars have debated (without much success) the precise identities of the lawless one and the one who restrains. The former seems to be an "antichrist" figure and is described as an agent of Satan (2:9). The image of him taking "his seat in the temple of God, declaring himself to be God" (2:4) is reminiscent of the emperor Caligula's attempt in A.D. 40 to have a statue of himself set up in the Jerusalem temple. The restrainer has been equated alternatively with the preaching of the gospel, the Roman Empire, or even God himself.

Jewish literature about the end of the world is full of mysterious, ill-defined future figures, such as the lawless one and the restrainer. Thus it is possible that the author of 2 Thessalonians had no specific characters in mind when he evoked these events and figures. Whatever their precise identities may have been, the point is that they represent a delay in Christ's second coming and the final judgment. Thus the author moves away from Paul's conviction that Christ will come "like a thief in the night"—that is, suddenly and without signs and warnings. Instead, he insists that certain events and figures must come first. Not only is the day of the Lord not already here (2:2), but it also has to go through a process that should be evident to all those with eyes to see.

The Problem of "Idleness." In 1 Thessalonians 5:14 Paul urged the Thessalonians to "admonish the idlers." The Greek adjective *ataktos* carries the sense of being disorderly or undisciplined. What was a small element in Paul's exhortation became a major topic in 2 Thessalonians 3:6–13. The reason seems to be that some Christians, out of the conviction that "the day of the Lord is already here" (2:2), were acting in disorderly ways and not contributing their fair share to the life of the community. The author's rule, "Anyone unwilling to work should not eat" (3:10), even made its way into the constitution of the Soviet Union.

The author points to the example of Paul, who in 1 Thessalonians 2:9 claimed that "we worked night and day, so that we might not burden any of you while we proclaimed to you the gospel of God." In 3:7–9 he adopts Paul's persona and reminds his readers that Paul insisted on supporting himself by his own labor rather than (rightfully) claiming support from the local Christian community. Paul was not an "idler," and neither should ordinary Christians be idlers. Rather, Christians should "do their work quietly and to earn their own living" (3:12).

Key Texts and Questions

Read 2 Thessalonians 1:5–10. Why do you think Paul included this material about the judgment at Christ's second coming?

Read 2:1–12. What should our attitude be about the second coming of Christ?

Read 3:6–15. If Paul were addressing your church, would idleness be the topic or can you name another issue he would need to confront?

He is the image of the invisible God, the firstborn of all creation; for in him all things in heaven and on earth were created, things visible and invisible, whether thrones or dominions or rulers or powers—all things have been created through him and for him. He himself is before all things, and in him all things hold together. He is the head of the body, the church; he is the beginning, the firstborn from the dead, so that he might come to have first place in everything. For in him all the fullness of God was pleased to dwell, and through him God was pleased to reconcile to himself all things, whether on earth or in heaven, by making peace through the blood of his cross.

—Colossians 1:15–20

The Letter to the Colossians

Colossae was a city in western Asia Minor (modern Turkey) about a hundred miles east of Ephesus. It was located in the upper Lycus River Valley, ten miles east of Laodicea and twelve miles southeast of Hierapolis. Colossae was regarded as an important city in the fifth century B.C. and later. But it was gradually outstripped by Laodicea and Hierapolis so that by the first century A.D. it was considered a smaller town. A severe earthquake in A.D. 60 or 61 may have contributed further to its decline.

The Christian community at Colossae was founded not by Paul directly but rather by Paul's coworker Epaphras (also known as Epaphroditus, see 1:7–8). From the lack of references to the Old Testament in this letter it seems that the Christians there were Gentile in background. However, according to the Roman writer Cicero there was a large Jewish population in the area (*Pro Flacco* 68). The letter to the Colossians, which was meant to be circulated in the neighboring cities (4:16), is best interpreted as a warning to Gentile Christians against the attractions of an esoteric Judaism, which may have taken over some elements from pagan philosophy and Greek mystery religions (2:8–23).

The letter to the Colossians is attributed to Paul and Timothy (1:1), though most of it is written in the first-person singular. If it was written directly by Paul, it must have been composed during one of his imprisonments for the sake of the gospel ("I am in prison," 4:3), perhaps at Caesarea Maritima or Rome—or even more likely at Ephesus, where he wrote to Philemon and the Philippians in the mid-50s of the first century.

Nevertheless, there are good reasons for supposing that the letter to the Colossians was written under Paul's name by an admirer who was somehow close to Paul. Keep in mind that the practice of imitating the style and thought of a famous author was *encouraged* in the schools of antiquity—to write such a document would not be considered dishonest or shameful. Our modern Western concepts of individual authorship and intellectual property were quite foreign to anyone's thinking then, except in the very highest literary circles. To write what Paul would have written in the new situation around A.D. 80 was a way of honoring Paul's memory and of demonstrating the vitality and adaptability of his thought.

The letter to the Colossians is very much in the spirit of Paul. It may have originated in the Pauline school based in Ephesus. It contains much from the language and theology of Paul. And it also seems to have addressed a real crisis (the attraction of Gentile Christians to an esoteric Judaism) in the churches of the Lycus River Valley region, if not at Colossae itself (which may have been in ruins due to the earthquake). This letter provided sound theological and pastoral advice to Gentile Christians there who were trying to figure out who they were as Christians in relation to the intellectual, spiritual, and social attractions of the local form of Judaism.

If Paul was not the author, we cannot be sure who was, beyond the fact that he was close to Paul. Timothy (1:1) and Epaphras (1:7–8) have been suggested. While the real author clearly admired and imitated Paul, he was not content merely to repeat what Paul thought and wrote. In several respects, while loyally following Paul, the author found his own distinctive theological voice. Instead of using the term "gospel," he prefers the word "mystery," which he links to the proclamation of Christ among the Gentiles (1:27). He stresses the universal and cosmic (rather than the end-times) significance of Christ (1:15–20), the present (rather than the future) dimension of salvation (2:11–13; 3:1), the church as a worldwide body (rather than the local community) with Christ as its head (1:18, 24; 2:19; 3:15), and Christian baptism (3:1–17) and good social order (3:18—4:1) as important reasons for Christian action (rather than expecting rewards at the last judgment).

The letter to the Colossians follows the usual outline of Paul's undisputed letters: greeting, thanksgiving and petition, the body of the letter consisting of doctrinal and ethical teachings, and concluding exhortations, travel plans, and related messages and greetings. If not composed by Paul himself, the letter to the Colossians is probably the earliest (around A.D. 80) example of the reception and adaptation of Paul's theology in the early church. Of course, the question of its authorship does not detract from the letter's status as Christian Scripture.

Overview of Colossians

Opening (1:1–2)
Thanksgiving and petition (1:3–11)
The lordship of Christ (1:12—2:23)
    Christ the Wisdom of God (1:12–23)
    Paul's ministry (1:24—2:5)
    Warnings (2:6–23)

Overview of Colossians, cont.
Christian life (3:1—4:6)
Foundations (3:1–4)
Vices and virtues (3:5–17)
Household code (3:18—4:1)
Prayer (4:2–6)
Messages and greetings (4:7–18)

Major Themes in This Letter

Christ the Wisdom of God. There is a consensus among biblical scholars that Colossians 1:15–20 contains an early Christian hymn about Christ as the Wisdom of God and about his role in the orders of creation and redemption. This consensus is based on the text's unusual vocabulary, parallel structures, and the rhythmic quality of its language. There is also a consensus that the hymn has been slightly modified in the process of its being incorporated into the letter. The identification of the "body" as the church in 1:18 and the reference to "the blood of his cross" in 1:20 help tie the hymn more directly to Christian church life and in baptismal rituals. That the hymn was originally used in the baptismal ceremony is suggested by the introduction in 1:12–14: "he has rescued us from the power of darkness and transferred us into the kingdom of his beloved Son." In the letter to the Colossians, the hymn functions as the key text to be developed and applied throughout the letter.

The first part of the hymn (1:15–18a) applies to Christ what is said about Wisdom in various Old Testament and early Jewish texts (Proverbs 8:22–36; Sirach 24; Wisdom 7; and *1 Enoch* 42:1–3). The same connection between Christ and Wisdom appears in John 1:1–18 and Hebrews 1:1–4. The hymn in Colossians 1 identifies Christ as the "image of the invisible God," as the agent and goal in God's creation of the world ("all things have been created through him and for him"), as the firstborn of all creation, and as the one who sustains all things. The implication is that there is no need to look elsewhere—even in forms of Judaism that claim to have secret knowledge—for the wisdom of God.

The second part (1:18b–20) takes its starting point from the resurrection of Christ ("the firstborn from the dead") and suggests that Christ is the one in whom all the fullness of God dwells and the one through whom God has brought about the reconciliation of the entire cosmos to God. By identifying the church as the body of Christ, with Christ as its head (1:18), the text links the risen Christ with the church. By insisting on "the blood of the cross" (1:20), the text affirms Paul's theology of the cross (1 Corinthians 1:18—2:5) and avoids any separation between the death and the resurrection of Jesus. What this means is that there is no need to look elsewhere for redemption and reconciliation with God—it was accomplished absolutely through Christ's death and resurrection.

Life in Christ. Christian life is based upon Christ's death and resurrection. The warnings against false philosophy were grounded in Jesus' death and resurrection (2:13b–15) and related to the believers' identification with them in baptism (2:11–13a, 20). Whereas those warnings were directed against a specific danger facing the community, the ethical teachings in 3:1—4:6 are less bound to a particular situation. They offer advice about vices to be avoided and virtues to be cultivated, as well as order in the household. Yet at nearly every point they remind us how Christian behavior relates to Jesus' death and resurrection.

The author draws parallels in 3:1–4 between Christ and believers on three counts:

> Christ has died, and we have died with him in
>   baptism.
> Christ has been raised, and we have been raised
>   with him in baptism.
> Christ will come again in glory, and we will
>   share in his glorious second coming. In the
>   meantime, between the present and Christ's
>   glorious second coming, our Christian life of
>   resurrection and glory remains "hidden with
>   Christ in God."

The claim of 3:1 is that believers have already been raised with Christ in baptism (2:12). While this goes beyond Romans 6:1–11, the assumption is still that the fullness of blessedness remains in the future. To seek "what is above" is to set one's mind and heart on the things of the spirit/Spirit and to orient one's life by them. The idea that Christ is now "seated at the right hand of God" alludes to Psalm 110:1, a text often cited in the New Testament to describe the exaltation of the risen Christ. The things "on earth" belong to the realm of what Paul characterizes as "the flesh."

The statement "you have died" in 3:3 refers to the notion of baptism as being buried with Christ (2:12, 20; Romans 6:1–11). The risen life of Christians, while certainly real, remains hidden "with Christ in God"—that is, not yet fully public—and Christians should set their minds and hearts on what is "above." At Christ's second coming (3:4, which is the only reference to it in Colossians), the resurrected life already enjoyed by Christians will become clear to all, as part of the glory displayed by Christ. Christians will also share in and enjoy the glory of God (Romans 8:18, 21, 30; 1 Thessalonians 2:12).

This theological reflection on Christ and baptism lays the theological foundation for the practical advice contained in the lists of vices and virtues that follow, as well as the household code.

The Household Code. In Colossians 3:18—4:1 we have the earliest example of a Christian "household code." The text describes the duties and obligations of the three pairs of persons who made up the ancient household: husbands and wives, fathers and children, and masters and slaves. In each case the author addresses the social inferior first and the social superior second. The first two units are brief, while the third unit (on slaves and masters) is quite long. The latter section may reflect attempts by Christian slaves to seek their freedom on the grounds that in Christ "there is no longer slave or free" (Galatians 3:28).

Much of the content of this household code embodies the cultural assumptions of the Greco-Roman world (see especially Aristotle's *Politics*) in the first century, including Jews in Palestine and scattered elsewhere, as well as early Christians. The Christian version accepts the social institutions of marriage, family, and slavery as givens and seeks to guide Christians on how to live within that conservative social framework. There is no direct attempt at reorganizing society according to other standards (Galatians 3:28). Any such attempt would surely have failed, given the small number of Christians then in the world and their very limited political influence.

Nevertheless, there are in 3:18—4:1 some subtle modifications of Greco-Roman social assumptions. Husbands and wives have mutual responsibilities to one another, and so there are limits on the husband's control over his wife. Fathers are urged to be sensitive to the feelings of their children. Even the institution of slavery is seen in a new light by the recognition that the ultimate master is Christ the Lord, and that Christ will exercise a final judgment upon both masters and slaves.

Two kinds of motivations run through this instruction. The first kind, rooted in the Greek cultural and philosophical tradition, grounds the directives in conforming to and preserving the good order of society: "as is fitting" (3:18), "this is your acceptable duty" (3:20), and "justly and fairly" (4:1). The second motivation is more clearly Christian: "in the Lord" (3:18, 20), "fearing the Lord" (3:22), "for the Lord" (3:23), "from the Lord" (3:24), and "you know that you also have a Master in heaven" (4:1). This combination of Jewish and Greco-Roman cultural values and Christian theological perspectives is typical of the moral teaching of the New Testament.

Key Texts and Questions

Read Colossians 1:15–20. In light of the hymn preserved in 1:15–20, what did early Christians believe about Jesus?

Read 3:1–4. Why is this passage an appropriate reading for Easter day?

Read 3:18—4:1. How do you react to the rules for Christian households covered in these verses?

You were dead through the trespasses and sins in which you once lived, following the course of this world, following the ruler of the power of the air, the spirit that is now at work among those who are disobedient. All of us once lived among them in the passions of our flesh, following the desires of flesh and senses, and we were by nature children of wrath, like everyone else. But God, who is rich in mercy, out of the great love with which he loved us even when we were dead through our trespasses, made us alive together with Christ—by grace you have been saved—and raised us up with him and seated us with him in the heavenly places in Christ Jesus, so that in the ages to come he might show the immeasurable riches of his grace in kindness toward us in Christ Jesus. For by grace you have been saved through faith, and this is not your own doing; it is the gift of God—not the result of works, so that no one may boast. For we are what he has made, created in Christ Jesus for good works, which God prepared beforehand to be our way of life.

—Ephesians 2:1–10

The Letter to the Ephesians

Ephesians reads more like an essay or treatise than a letter. It purports to come from Paul and is addressed to "the saints who are in Ephesus" (1:1). However, the words "in Ephesus" are absent from some very early manuscripts. The letter is quite general in expression and tone, and it does not appear to respond to any specific crisis in the local church. It reflects on the "mystery" of the church comprised of Jews and Gentiles, and offers advice about Christian life. Its author knew the letter to the Colossians and used it most obviously in the household code in 5:21—6:9 but also throughout the letter (Ephesians 2:5–6 = Colossians 2:12 and Ephesians 3:2–10 = Colossians 1:25–29). Whereas the focus of Colossians was Christ, Ephesians is particularly interested in the church as the body of Christ.

Those who defend the direct Pauline authorship of Ephesians regard it as a mature statement written by the apostle as a prisoner for the gospel (6:20), shortly before his death. But there are good reasons for viewing Ephesians as Deuteropauline. Although deeply indebted to Paul in language and style, the author of Ephesians prefers long sentences and uses many words not found in Paul's undisputed letters. Also, the author is more concerned with the universal church than with individual local churches, and he identifies the apostles and prophets as the foundation of the church (2:20) rather than Christ as the foundation, which is what Paul did (1 Corinthians 3:11). The writer defines the "mystery" of God's plan as the coming together of Jews and Gentiles to form the "one new humanity" in Christ (Ephesians 2:15). In 5:22–33 he offers a high view of marriage and encourages it rather than allowing it as a mere concession as Paul did (1 Corinthians 7:6). He stresses the exaltation of Christ and refers only once to the cross (2:16) and the resurrection (1:20) and never refers to the second coming of Christ.

Ephesians may well have been conceived as an official document to be circulated among the churches of Asia Minor (present-day Turkey). Its connection with Colossians points to such a setting. Its vision of reconciliation between Jews and Gentiles in 2:11–22 suggests that Paul's problem with the Christian Judaizers (as in Galatians, Philippians, and 2 Corinthians) was in the past, and marks a new development even beyond Romans 9—11. It seems most likely that this letter was composed in the 80s or 90s of the first century A.D..

Overview of Ephesians

Opening (1:1–2)

Blessing (1:3–14)

Thanksgiving (1:15–23)

The mystery of God's plan (2:1—3:21)

　　From death to life (2:1–10)

　　Jews and Gentiles in Christ (2:11–22)

　　Paul's ministry (3:1–13)

　　Prayer and doxology (3:14–21)

Life in Christ (4:1—6:20)

　　Unity in the body of Christ (4:1–16)

　　Old life and new life (4:17–24)

　　Rules for new life (4:25—5:20)

　　Household code (5:21—6:9)

　　The armor of God (6:10–20)

Commendation of Tychicus, and farewell prayer
　　(6:21–24)

Major Themes in This Letter

Blessings in Christ. After the greeting (1:1–2), Ephesians presents a long and involved benediction (1:3–14). It blesses God for blessing us in Christ "with every spiritual blessing," and goes on to list the benefits flowing from Jesus' life, death, resurrection, and exaltation. Here the author's focus is on how Christ's death and resurrection benefit us, his followers.

These benefits include:

election to be holy and blameless before God;

adoption as children of God;

redemption and forgiveness of sins;

knowledge of the "mystery" of God's will;

enjoyment of the inheritance promised to us, and

the gift of the Holy Spirit as the pledge of our

redemption "as God's own people."

At every point there is mention of Christ's involvement with us ("in Christ . . . through Jesus Christ . . . through his blood"); in this way, the opening of the letter introduces the reader to themes about the people of God and the body of Christ to be developed in chapters 2 and 3.

People of God and Body of Christ. In 2:11–22 the author describes how Christ forms the people made up of Jewish and Gentile Christians. To do so, he applies the pattern "at one time . . . but now in Christ Jesus" on a community scale in describing the state of humankind before and apart from Christ and the new state of humanity brought about through Christ.

The author begins in 2:11–12 by reminding the Gentile Christians ("the uncircumcision") that "at one time" they were separated from Christ and from the privileges and promises made by God to Israel as his people. Then in 2:13–18 he shows how Christ has broken down the "dividing wall" between Jews and Gentiles and has made them into the "one new humanity." In 2:16 his reference to Christ as having reconciled "both groups to God in one body through the cross" is both to the crucified body of Christ through which reconciliation with God has been made possible and to the church as Christ's body and the place of Christ's power (1:22–23). The body of Christ has made Jews and Gentiles into the people of God.

Other aspects of this new entity are expressed in 2:19–22 with the images of the church as the "household of God," "a holy temple in the Lord," and "a dwelling place for God." And in 5:22–33 the author rewrites and greatly expands the section of the household code about husbands and wives (Colossians 3:18–19) into a meditation on the loving relationship between Christ and his church.

The Mystery. Like Paul in Romans 9—11, the author of Ephesians sought to explain how non-Jews could become part of the people of God. Like Paul, his answer was, through Christ. But while Paul was greatly concerned with part of Israel's present unbelief and hoped that in the end "all Israel will be saved" (Romans 11:26), the author of Ephesians ignores the future of unbelieving Israel and is concerned primarily with the present state of the church composed of Jews and Gentiles. Whereas Paul (Romans 11:25–26) defined the "mystery" of God's plan in terms of the hardening of some in Israel, the admission of the full number of Gentiles into God's people, and the ultimate salvation of all Israel, the author of Ephesians redefines the mystery in this way: "the Gentiles have become fellow heirs, members of the same body, and sharers in the promise in Christ Jesus through the gospel" (3:6).

The Armor of God. Most of Ephesians 4—6 concerns the attitudes and behaviors that are consistent with the new life that Christians now enjoy in Christ. As a way of summarizing his approach to Christian life, the author in 6:10–17 evokes the imagery of an ancient soldier preparing for battle. But this is no ordinary war. Here the combat is spiritual, and the enemy is the devil. (The devil or Satan is not a prominent figure in Paul's undisputed letters, where sin, death, and the Law are stressed and personified.)

The armor that the Christian needs is not material but spiritual: the belt of truth, the breastplate of righteousness, shoes for proclaiming the gospel, the shield of faith to deflect the devil's arrows, the helmet of salvation, and the sword of the Spirit "which is the word of God." These weapons and pieces of equipment will enable the Christian to triumph over "the cosmic powers of this present darkness" (6:12).

Key Texts and Questions

Read 2:11–22. What might it mean to your own community if Christians took to heart what Paul is saying in this passage?

Read 3:1–13. Why was Paul called to preach Christ to the Gentiles?

These are the things you must insist on and teach. Let no one despise your youth, but set the believers an example in speech and conduct, in love, in faith, in purity. Until I arrive, give attention to the public reading of scripture, to exhorting, to teaching. Do not neglect the gift that is in you, which was given to you through prophecy with the laying on of hands by the council of elders. Put these things into practice, devote yourself to them, so that all may see your progress. Pay close attention to yourself and to your teaching; continue in these things, for in doing this you will save both yourself and your hearers.

—1 Timothy 4:11–16

The First Letter to Timothy

The letters to Timothy and Titus are known as the "pastoral epistles," because they are addressed to the chief pastors at Ephesus (Timothy) and Crete (Titus), and they concern the pastoral problems and duties in those local communities.

Those who defend their direct Pauline authorship point to their many personal details and contend that they were written late in Paul's life—that is, in the early 60s. Those who deny their direct Pauline authorship attribute them to an admirer or follower of Paul toward the end of the first century A.D. or even later. They explain the personal details as a tactic of imitation. They point to the different vocabulary and style from the undisputed letters of Paul and to emphases more appropriate to conditions in the late first century than to Paul's own time in the mid-first century. These emphases include faith as a formulated body of doctrines (the "deposit" of faith), the sharp line between sound doctrine and false teaching, local church officials as the guardians of good order and sound doctrine, and respectability and good example as the most effective missionary strategy.

First Timothy and Titus treat many of these topics and give the impression of small units pieced together, while 2 Timothy is a more integrated personal statement or testament from Paul as he faces the prospect of his death. The similarities in style and content give the impression of composition by a single author, whether it was Paul himself or a later admirer.

The background of 1 Timothy is that on Paul's way to Macedonia he left Timothy in Ephesus where he was supposed to "instruct certain people not to teach any different doctrine" (1:3). Thus the letter advises Timothy on what to emphasize and how to bring better order into the Christian community there.

What exactly the false teachers were saying and doing is not entirely clear, though according to 4:1–5 they forbade marriage and demanded abstinence from certain foods. In response to their teaching, the letter supplies several already traditional formulations of Christian faith, which are often accompanied by affirmations of their truth. For example, "the saying is sure and worthy of full acceptance, that Christ Jesus came into the world to save sinners" (1:15; see also 2:5–6; 3:16).

Overview of 1 Timothy

Opening (1:1–2)

Warning against false teachers (1:3–20)

Order in the assembly (2:1–15)

Bishops and deacons (3:1–13)

The mystery of our religion (3:14–16)

False asceticism (4:1–5)

Advice to Timothy (4:6—5:2)

Widows (5:3–17)

Elders (5:18–25)

Slaves and Masters (6:1–2)

False teaching and true riches (6:3–10)

Overview of 1 Timothy, cont.
Advice to Timothy (6:11–19)
Closing (6:20–21)

Major Themes in This Letter

Women. Whereas Paul assumes that women pray and prophesy in the Christian assembly (1 Corinthians 11:2–16), the author of 1 Timothy takes a more restrictive approach to women's participation and permits "no woman to teach or to have authority over a man" (2:12). He also insists on modesty in women's attire, blames the "original sin" more on Eve than on Adam, and claims that women will be saved through childbearing (2:9–15). While these statements are hard to defend in any age, they may reflect efforts to combat false teachers who forbade marriage (4:3); they may also have been intended to make the Christian community appear more respectable to outsiders in a highly patriarchal society. By contrast, the letter also presents in 5:3–16 a detailed program for the care of Christian widows left without any means of support.

Church Officers. The Pastorals—1 and 2 Timothy, and Titus— bear witness to a moment in early Christian history when the traveling apostles such as Paul were receding in their prominence and local church leaders were becoming more crucial to the lives

of the faithful. First Timothy provides lists of the personal qualities and virtues that bishops (3:1–7) and deacons (3:8–13) should
possess. The mention of women in 3:11 suggests that they could
hold the office of deacon. The precise relationship between the
two offices is not clear. Both lists place emphasis on good order
and a respectable reputation among outsiders. In particular, since
the church is "the household of God" (3:15), all of them must
display the characteristics that will enable them to manage their
own household successfully. The implication is that these bishops
and deacons will be married persons.

The picture of church officers is further complicated by mention of elders or presbyters in 5:17–22. Those elders who also
preached and taught are said to be "worthy of double honor"
(5:17). There is also reference to elders being accused of misconduct and the chilling warning to Timothy, "Do not ordain
anyone hastily" (5:22). How the office of elder/presbyter fit with
those of bishop and deacon is not explained. Indeed, some scholars suggest that these three offices reflect two different historical and cultural patterns—the Jewish synagogues (elders) and the
Greco-Roman voluntary associations (bishops and deacons), and
that these two patterns had not yet come together to form the
bishop-priest (elder/presbyter)-deacon hierarchy that emerged in
the second century.

Key Texts and Questions

Read 1 Timothy 3:1–13. What qualifications are most important for bishops, priests, and deacons today? What roles should women have in the church?

Read 6:11–16. What might fighting "the good fight of the faith" mean for you personally?

In a large house there are utensils not only of gold and silver but also of wood and clay, some for special use, some for ordinary. All who cleanse themselves of the things I have mentioned will become special utensils, dedicated and useful to the owner of the house, ready for every good work. Shun youthful passions and pursue righteousness, faith, love, and peace along with those who call on the Lord from a pure heart. Have nothing to do with stupid and senseless controversies; you know that they breed quarrels. And the Lord's servant must not be quarrelsome but kindly to everyone, an apt teacher, patient, correcting opponents with gentleness. God may perhaps grant that they will repent and come to know the truth, and that they may escape from the snare of the devil, having been held captive by him to do his will.

—2 Timothy 2:20–26

The Second Letter to Timothy

In the scenario of 2 Timothy, Paul writes from prison in Rome (1:8, 16–17). He has been through one trial and awaits another, and he expects to be martyred (4:6–8). As he nears the end of his life, he writes to his longtime coworker, Timothy, at Ephesus and offers him advice and encouragement. He also hopes that Timothy will visit him before winter (4:21).

This letter contains many personal details and takes the form of a testament or farewell discourse. Those who defend its direct Pauline authorship view 2 Timothy as Paul's spiritual "last will and testament" to an old friend and as a set of directives for all who seek to carry on Paul's apostolic legacy. Those who regard it as only written in Paul's name place it in the late first or early second century A.D., perhaps at Ephesus (which seems to have been the location of a Pauline "school"). They explain the personal details as a convention of literary imitation, which was common at the time. They also point to the inner-church conflicts noted in the letter as fitting better in the period after Paul's death than in the late 50s or early 60s of the first century.

Among theologians, 2 Timothy 3:16 has often been quoted in debates about the inspiration and authority of Scripture: "All scripture is inspired by God and is useful for teaching." In the context of 2 Timothy, the "scripture" here must be the Old Testament, since it is doubtful that the writings now known as the New Testament were yet regarded as "Scripture."

> **Overview of 2 Timothy**
> Opening (1:1–2)
> Thanksgiving (1:3–5)
> Suffering for the gospel (1:6–14)
> Paul's situation (1:15–17)
> Expect suffering (2:1–13)
> Beware of false teachers (2:14–26)
> Signs of the end-time (3:1–9)
> Paul's example (3:10—4:8)
> Paul's situation (4:9–15)
> Paul's trials (4:16–18)
> Final greetings and prayers (4:19–22)

Major Themes in This Letter

Paul's Example. In the literary form we know as the *testament*, the dying hero looks back on his life and draws lessons from it. He looks forward into the future and offers challenges and hopes to the listeners or readers. In Paul's farewell letter to Timothy, he emphasizes his own sufferings for the sake of the gospel, and he warns Timothy (and all readers) to expect similar sufferings in carrying on the ministry.

Paul defines the gospel as "Jesus Christ, raised from the dead, a descendant of David" (2:8). He recalls his own sufferings for the gospel in Antioch, Iconium, and Lystra (3:11), and his disappointments with some of his coworkers (4:16). Nevertheless, when compared to the overwhelming value of his commission to spread the gospel, Paul's sufferings and persecution seem to be of minor importance. Paul accepts them with an eye toward the greater good—that the elect may "obtain the salvation that is in Christ Jesus, with eternal glory" (2:10) and with perfect trust in God's faithfulness (2:13). Thus he approaches death with the composure and confidence of one who fully expects to enjoy eternal life with God and Christ: "I have fought the good fight, I have finished the race, I have kept faith" (4:7).

Conflict within the Church. Paul's instruction in these pastoral letters involves a good deal of turmoil within Christian communities. Much of the language is vague: "wrangling over words . . . profane chatter" (2:14, 16). However, there is a specific accusation against Hymenaeus and Philetus for "claiming that the resurrection has already taken place" (2:18). These two men may have been propagating a theology in which we already enjoy the fullness of resurrected life. Paul insisted that baptism and the gift of the Holy Spirit were only the first installment toward the fullness of life with God. In 3:1–9 there is another accusation against false teachers in which the author accuses them of targeting "silly women" (3:6). That may help to explain the negative comments about women and the insistence on their subordination to their husbands in 1 Timothy 2:11–15.

Key Texts and Questions

Read 3:1–9 and 4:1–8. How do these descriptions of corrupted faith apply to the situations around you? How would you say, in today's terms, what Paul is saying here to Timothy?

Remind them to be subject to rulers and authorities, to be obedient, to be ready for every good work, to speak evil of no one, to avoid quarreling, to be gentle, and to show every courtesy to everyone. For we ourselves were once foolish, disobedient, led astray, slaves to various passions and pleasures, passing our days in malice and envy, despicable, hating one another. But when the goodness and loving kindness of God our Savior appeared, he saved us, not because of any works of righteousness that we had done, but according to his mercy, through the water of rebirth and renewal by the Holy Spirit. This Spirit he poured out on us richly through Jesus Christ our Savior, so that, having been justified by his grace, we might become heirs according to the hope of eternal life.

—Titus 3:1–7

The Letter to Titus

The scenario of the letter to Titus places Paul in Nicopolis in Greece (3:12) and writing to his coworker Titus on Crete (1:5). Titus's task is to put the church there "in order" by appointing elders/presbyters, combating false teachers, clarifying what was expected of various community members, and urging all to exemplary conduct in the hope of gaining more converts.

Those who believe that Paul wrote this letter place its writing sometime during his journey to Rome (Acts 27), and thus late in his career. Those who consider it written in Paul's name by a later author point to its emphases on sound doctrine, local church leaders, order in the church, Greek philosophical language, and exemplary conduct as indications that it was written in the late first century A.D. In other words, these are issues Paul would have written about had he still been alive during that period.

Overview of Titus

Opening (1:1–4)

Elders and bishops (1:5–9)

False teachers (1:10–16)

Order in the Community (2:1–10)

God's will to save (2:11–15)

Christians in society (3:1–8)

Avoiding false teachers (3:9–11)

Final messages and blessing (3:12–15)

Major Themes in This Letter

Order in the Community. The first thing that Titus is told to do on Crete is to appoint presbyters and bishops. It's not clear whether the plan is for one office or two. The task of these leaders is to oversee the community's life, and so they must be respectable and virtuous. They also need a good grasp of "sound doctrine" to be able to refute the false teachers.

The household code in 2:1–10 notes the virtues most appropriate for various members of a Christian household and for the church as the household of God: older men and women, younger men and women, and slaves. Again the emphasis is on outward respectability and good order. Titus himself must be a model of good works and able to avoid scandal. It's clear from this emphasis on behavior and respect in the community that the most effective missionary strategy is the good example of Christians. It also appears that Christians are becoming increasingly integrated into the Greco-Roman world, and that the focus of missionary activity is shifting to building up strong local communities.

Inculturation. The postscript to the household code in 2:11–14 combines words and concepts from different backgrounds, and so is a good example of inculturation—that is, the church integrating the gospel into the Greco-Roman world. It begins with general Christian theological language: "For the grace of God has appeared, bringing salvation to all" (2:11). Next, in 2:12, it recommends the cultivation of the Greek philosophical virtues ("self-controlled, upright, and godly"). Then in 2:13 the language echoes and challenges Roman imperial propaganda: "the manifestation of the glory of our great God and Savior, Jesus Christ." Finally in 2:14 we hear more distinctively Pauline language: "who gave himself for us that he might redeem us from all iniquity and purify for himself a people of his own who are zealous for good deeds." This passage provides a Christian theological rationale for good order and virtuous living in a way that made the gospel intelligible and attractive to people in the late first-century Greco-Roman world.

Key Texts and Questions

Read Titus 1:5–9. What qualities would you most hope for in a pastor?

Read 2:1–10. How would you make the advice here real and applicable in today's setting?

Read 3:4–7. In the midst of all the troubles and challenges of ministry, of what does the writer remind Titus and the other believers?

4

How Might We Interpret a Pauline Text Today?

The material in this chapter is structured around one short New Testament passage, Romans 8:26–27. We will use this passage to answer three basic questions about reading Paul:

> How do modern biblical interpreters approach their
> sacred texts?
> How can biblical texts shape Christian thinking?
> How might biblical scholarship flow naturally into
> the spiritual lives of people of faith?

The methods illustrated in this chapter can be applied to any passage in the outlines of the Pauline letters discussed in the body of this book.

Text and Translations

To illustrate the process of Christian biblical interpretation, I've chosen Romans 8:26–27 for several reasons: It is short; it is theologically rich and personally meaningful to me; and it comes from the apostle Paul—certainly one of the most influential and controversial figures in Christian history.

I will deal with this text on three levels—literary, historical, and theological.

First, however, I will present two current and widely used English translations of this text so that we know from the start what the text says. All the books of the New Testament were composed in Greek—a kind of Greek called *Koine*, or "Common"—and heavily influenced by the Jewish Greek version of the Hebrew Bible known as the Septuagint. The most famous and influential English translation has been the King James Version (1611). In recent years, however, we have seen the publication of many new translations that in various circles have replaced the King James Version.

The first translation of Romans 8:26–27 is from the *New American Bible* (revised, 1986), an American Catholic translation in which several Protestant scholars played major roles:

> 26 In the same way, the Spirit too comes to the aid of our weakness; for we do not know how to pray as we ought, but the Spirit itself intercedes with inexpressible groanings. 27 And the one who searches hearts knows what is the intention of the Spirit, because it intercedes for the holy ones according to God's will.

The second translation is from the *New Revised Standard Version* (1990), historically an American Protestant translation to which Catholic and Jewish scholars have made important contributions:

26 Likewise the Spirit helps us in our weakness; for
we do not know how to pray as we ought, but that
very Spirit intercedes with sighs too deep for words.
27 And God, who searches the heart, knows what is
the mind of the Spirit, because the Spirit intercedes
for the saints according to the will of God.

One could add translations from the British Catholic *New
Jerusalem Bible*, the British Protestant *Revised English Bible*, the
Evangelical *New International Version*, and the United Bible
Societies' *Good News Bible*. All are good and reliable translations,
when we take account of their distinctive translation philosophies
and the purposes for which they were produced.

Comparison of two (or more) translations can help alert careful
readers to some problems in the text. Is the Holy Spirit an "it" or a
"he" (or a "she")? Is there a difference between "inexpressible groanings" and "sighs too deep for words?" Who "searches hearts"—
God or someone else? Does the Holy Spirit have an "intention" or a
"mind"? Is it "holy ones" or "saints" for whom the Spirit intercedes?
The multiplicity of translations can thus be viewed as a way of rais-
ing preliminary questions about the text and as an aid in exploring
its richness, rather than as a threat or a nuisance.

Literary Analysis

In interpreting a biblical text by way of literary analysis, we must
attend to its context, words and images, characters, structure,
and form. Attention to context is the natural first step in literary

analysis. Romans 8:26–27 occurs roughly in the middle of Paul's letter to the Romans—in what is arguably the most important chapter in the most important book in the Christian Bible. Paul wrote to the Roman Christians in the mid-fifties of the first century. Paul's practical goal in writing this letter was to help Jewish Christians and Gentile Christians in Rome look upon one another as equals before God through Christ. The main topic of the letter is the gospel, which, for Paul, meant the saving significance of Jesus' death and resurrection. So Paul's letter to the Romans deals with the nature of the gospel, the need for the gospel, the gospel and faith, the gospel and freedom, the gospel and life in the Spirit, the gospel and the mystery of salvation, the gospel and Christian life, the gospel and conflict, and the promotion of the gospel.

Thus Romans 8:26–27 is part of Paul's meditation on life in the Spirit. The word "spirit" (*pneuma*) is itself ambiguous. The earliest Greek manuscripts are written entirely in capital letters, and so we can judge the meaning only by the context. When spelled in English with a small "s," it refers to that aspect of the human person that is receptive and open to God (as opposed to the "flesh"). When spelled with a capital "S," it refers to what we call the Holy Spirit—the Spirit of God.

After describing how the Holy Spirit empowers a person to live in the "Spirit" (8:1–11), Paul explains how Christians can be called children of God (8:12–17), reflects on the present-future and individual-cosmic dimensions of Christian spirituality (8:18–25), presents teachings on the role of the Holy Spirit in prayer (8:26–27), and develops the affirmation that God is for us and with us (8:28–39).

The second step in literary analysis is to attend to the words and images that make up the text. Romans 8:26 identifies the Holy Spirit as the primary agent in prayer. This Spirit of God works with, and especially through, human "weakness"—a way of expressing the unfinished or "not yet" aspect of Christ's redemptive work, and the lingering effects of the power of sin and death. The "inexpressible groanings" or "sighs too deep for words" that accompany prayer are both a sign of human weakness and a proof that the intercession of the Holy Spirit is needed.

In Romans 8:27 "the one who searches hearts" is most likely God who works in tandem with the Holy Spirit (see below). An alternate interpretation takes the Holy Spirit as the one who searches hearts and so has the "Spirit" working with the human "spirit." The terms "holy ones" and "saints" were commonly applied to the early Christians (as well as to members of the Dead Sea sect). They refer first of all to God as the Holy One who communicates holiness to human beings, thus enabling them to be called "holy ones."

There are three main characters in Romans 8:26–27: the Holy Spirit, those who pray, and God. The Spirit helps those who pray and makes sure that God hears their prayers. The literary structure proceeds as follows: a general affirmation about the Spirit and human weakness (8:26a), an application of this idea to prayer (8:26b), and a statement about how the three main characters work together (8:27). In form, the passage is one part of Paul's meditative exposition of life in the spirit/Spirit.

Historical Analysis

In interpreting a biblical text by historical analysis, we must attend to its tradition history, ancient parallels, and concrete life-setting. The expression "the one who searches hearts" reflects a rich biblical tradition. In the Hebrew Scriptures it clearly refers to God, and appears in various forms (1 Samuel 16:7; 1 Kings 8:39; 1 Chronicles 28:9; and Psalms 7:9; 17:3; 139:1). According to those passages, God looks into the human heart, studies and knows the heart, and searches and tests the hearts of humankind. God knows us better than we know ourselves.

Some interesting parallels to the insistence in Romans 8:26–27 that the Holy Spirit helps humans in their prayer can be found in the *Thanksgiving Hymns* among the Dead Sea Scrolls at Qumran. The best example occurs in column 8 (formerly 16), lines 11–13, where the speaker prays to God: "And I know that no one is righteous apart from you, and I implore you by the spirit that you have given me to make perfect your mercies with your servant forever and ever, to purify me by your holy spirit, and to draw me near by your grace according to the greatness of your mercies." While the speaker does not mean by "holy spirit" exactly what Paul meant (Paul's concept of holy spirit has been transformed by the person of Jesus Christ), he does acknowledge the need for the help of God's holy spirit in prayer ("I implore you by the spirit that you have given me") in the light of human weakness ("no one is righteous apart from you")—just as Paul does. I doubt that Paul read this particular Qumran text. More likely it is a case of independent expressions of the same basic idea by two Jewish writers from roughly the same time.

Some interpreters find in the phrase "inexpressible groanings" a clue to the concrete life-setting of Romans 8:26–27. They
see in it an allusion to speaking in tongues—a phenomenon discussed at length in 1 Corinthians 12—14. Whereas some early
Christians regarded this prayer experience as the greatest spiritual
gift, Paul sought to play down its importance because without
interpretation it did not build up the community and contrib-
ute to the spiritual progress of the other members. Speaking
in tongues most likely took the form not of foreign languages
(despite Acts 2) but rather of wordless vocal expressions ("grunts
and groans"). And so it is possible (though not all commentators
agree) to find in "inexpressible groanings" another put-down of
those who prided themselves on speaking in tongues. Instead of
being a sign of spiritual virtuosity, these "inexpressible groanings"
would signify, according to Paul, human weakness in prayer and
the need for the Holy Spirit to help in addressing God so that the
prayer might be understood properly.

Theological Analysis

Besides literary and historical analysis, Christian biblical interpretation involves theological reflection. Romans 8:26–27 is a rich
theological text. With its references to God and the Holy Spirit
and in the context of the letter as a whole with its basic theme of
what God has done in and through Jesus' death and resurrection,
the passage makes important contributions to the doctrine of the
Trinity. And it contains many beautiful subthemes: our human
weakness before God, God as the one who searches hearts,

Christians as "holy ones," and so forth. But the chief theological theme is prayer—what we do when we pray, and what God and the Holy Spirit do when we pray. This theme emerges naturally out of the literary and historical study, and at the same time cries out to be made real, or current, in a community of faith.

Reading an Old Text in a New Situation

The term "actualization" describes the process of reading ancient texts in new circumstances and applying them to the current situation of the people of God. It is an old process. In the Hebrew Scriptures, Israel's return from exile in Babylon was interpreted in Isaiah 40—55 in the light of the exodus and creation traditions. In the Dead Sea Scrolls (especially the biblical commentaries) the texts of the Prophets and Psalms were explained in terms of the Qumran sect's life and history. The New Testament church read the Jewish Scriptures through their belief in Christ and all that was promised and fulfilled through him. The commentaries of the rabbis and of the Church Fathers are at root examples of actualization. When Christians today pray over the Scriptures, engage in Bible-study groups, and teach and preach on the basis of biblical texts, they, too, engage in the process of actualization.

One ancient, simple, and recently revived way of actualization is the method of prayer based on the Scriptures known as *lectio divina* ("divine," or spiritual, reading). It starts with a short passage of Scripture such as Romans 8:26–27 and then works through four basic exercises developed out of four questions:

Reading: What does the text say?

Meditation: What does the text say to me?

Prayer: What do I say to God through this text?

Contemplation and/or action: What difference
    might this text make in my life?

Through the literary, historical, and theological analysis on Romans 8:26–27 that we've already done, we've accomplished the first exercise and answered the first question. The remaining three exercises are quite personal, but they are essential to making the scripture passage "actual" to our current time, place, and situation.

The tradition of contemplative prayer developed by Ignatius Loyola, the founder of the Jesuits, can enrich this method. Ignatius insisted that people enter a biblical passage imaginatively, using their physical senses and identifying with the characters in the passage. So in contemplating Romans 8:26–27 a person might envision an early Christian assembly and ask: What do I see? What do I hear? What do I smell? Or the person doing this exercise might identify with an ancient tongue-speaker, and consider how he might have evaluated his spiritual gift. This would lead to considering the person's own spiritual gifts (or lack thereof), and to meditating on the Holy Spirit as the source of these gifts.

These methods of biblically based prayer can be extended to more public forums. Bible-study groups meet regularly in Christian communities both to understand the biblical texts and to use them as spiritual resources. They range in goals and practice from focusing on what the text meant in its original historical setting to what it might mean in people's lives today, with most groups combining those two questions. Some are satisfied with gathering information about the ancient texts, while others use them to discuss current affairs, to facilitate group prayer, or to inspire dramatic or artistic expressions.

In religious education, the biblical texts read at the Sunday liturgy are often taken as the starting point for study and discussion by people of all ages. And of course the Christian Liturgy of the Word revolves around biblical texts, and provides for the most obvious way of Scripture actualization—the sermon or homily, which is supposed to be first and foremost the exposition and actualization of a biblical text.

A Sample "Actualization": Romans 8:26–27

What follows is a homily on Romans 8:26–27 that moves from the scholarly analysis of the biblical text that we have already done to a reflection that tries to help Christians today realize what we do when we pray. It makes a point that is very important to me personally and that others have found encouraging and helpful in their prayer.

> "Likewise the Spirit helps us in our weakness; for we do not know how to pray as we ought" (Romans 8:26a). An essential element in Christian spirituality is prayer. In fact, we tend to equate spirituality and

prayer. Most of us can define prayer. It is the lifting of the heart and mind to God. We can distinguish the different kinds of prayer: praise, adoration, thanksgiving, and petition. We know the various forms of prayer: song, meditation, contemplation, and so forth. We can recite certain prayers from memory. We enter into the official prayer of the church by participating in the sacrament of the Eucharist and other liturgies. We know a lot about prayer.

And yet, most serious religious people come away from their prayer aware of their fundamental inadequacy before God. There is so much we want to express to God in our prayer—our reverence, our thankfulness, and our love. And yet the words we use seem so inadequate, and the forms we use seem so flimsy and weak. And so the problem that Paul touches on in this biblical text is our problem too: "We do not know how to pray as we ought."

Paul's answer can be our answer too. Paul's answer is that the ground of genuine Christian spirituality is the Holy Spirit, that true prayer is a gift from God, and that the Holy Spirit helps us in our weakness. Prayer is not something that we do entirely on our own. Rather, prayer is something that the Holy Spirit does through us. That is the most profound and comforting insight about prayer that I know: Prayer is something that the Holy Spirit does through us.

In our prayer, according to Paul, the Holy Spirit does two basic things: (1) The Holy Spirit helps us express what we want to say to God. (2) The Holy Spirit helps God—the one who searches hearts— understand what we say when we pray.

First, the Holy Spirit helps us express what we want to say to God. The God we approach in prayer is the one we believe to be the Creator and Sustainer of all things. For us to speak to this God seems pretentious at best and blasphemous at worst. Who are we to speak to the Lord of the universe? What can we say that God does not already know? How can we speak to God in an appropriate manner? All our words are too small. All our phrases are inadequate. Sometimes the best we can do is a groan or a sigh or a cry—something that expresses our inmost longing and love for God. And this is precisely Paul's point: "The Spirit too comes to the aid of our weakness." When we pray from the heart, when we pray the prayer that goes beyond mere human words and external forms, it is the Spirit who prays through us. As I said before, this is the most profound and comforting teaching on prayer that I know.

Second, the Holy Spirit helps God the Father of us all—the one who searches hearts—to understand what we say when we pray. The point here is not that the Holy Spirit is entirely separate from God, or that the Father really needs help. Rather, the point concerns us: How can we be sure that God understands what we say in our prayer? The answer is simply this: The Spirit makes sure that our prayers are understood, that the deepest feelings of our heart—our groans, sighs, and cries—are properly interpreted by God.

From beginning to end, the Holy Spirit is involved in our prayer. The Holy Spirit helps us formulate our prayers. The Holy Spirit makes sure that our prayers are heard and understood. In our prayer we are not alone. Indeed, in our prayer we are not even the principal agent. The Holy Spirit is the principal agent in our prayer, and we cooperate with the Holy Spirit.

Christian spirituality is not "do it yourself" spirituality. Rather, it is a response to the grace of God and to the promptings of the Holy Spirit. Even in the most obvious exercise of Christian spirituality—prayer—the action of God comes first. In our prayer we become aware of and acknowledge our weakness. At the same time we also recognize that the Holy Spirit helps us in our weakness. From beginning to end the Holy Spirit is involved in our prayer. Those are the most profound and comforting teachings about prayer and Christian life that I know. And they are vintage Pauline theology. Amen!

5

What Can We Learn from Paul Today?

As we move further into the third millennium of Christian history, Paul the apostle stands not only as a great figure of the past but also as a guide to the present and future of the church. Many of Paul's problems are our problems, and many of Paul's answers can and should be our answers, too.

The Paul who emerges from the pages of the New Testament is a somewhat angular character. He is energetic, committed, enthusiastic, and often heroic. But he sometimes also appears as driven, defensive, sarcastic, and even nasty. His opponents dismissed him as weak in bodily presence and contemptible in speech, though they admitted that he could write good letters (2 Corinthians 10:10). He was controversial and attracted fierce opposition. Paul was no plaster saint. His greatness resided in his passion for the gospel of Jesus Christ and his desire to share it with others.

The church of the twenty-first century can learn much from Paul. We can learn about the sad state of humankind before and apart from Christ, under the sway of sin, death, and the Law. We can learn how Jesus' death and resurrection have changed everything and made possible a new and better relationship with God (justification). And we can learn about baptism as the sacrament by which we come to share in the saving action of Jesus.

We can learn about the church as the body of Christ and the people of God, and about our continuing relationship with the Jewish people. We can learn that each Christian has been gifted by the Holy Spirit and must use those gifts for the common good and so build up the body of Christ. We can learn to appreciate better the Eucharist or Lord's Supper as the sacrament of ongoing Christian life, and that we all stand as equals before God in the Christian community.

We can learn to recognize the prominence of women in Paul's mission and ministry, and the high value that Paul placed on collaborative ministry. We can learn about our everyday lives as the locus of our worship of God and about the importance of acting in ways that fit who we are as Christians. We can learn about the value of order and structure in Christian community life as a means of directing our spiritual energies into words and actions that edify those in the church and those outside it. And we can learn about the balance between our present blessedness (the first fruits of the Spirit) and the future "freedom of the glory of the children of God" (Romans 8:21).

We can learn from the personal example of Paul who supported his own ministry, suffered for the gospel, and shared the good news "like a nurse tenderly caring for her own children" (1 Thessalonians 2:7). We can learn from Paul the pastoral theologian, who dealt with the real problems of his fellow Christians in the light of the gospel, and who developed his theology in relation to his work as a pastor. Most of all, we can learn from Paul's own declaration about his experience of Jesus' death and resurrection and about his greatest hope: "I want to know Christ and the power of his resurrection and the sharing of his sufferings by becoming like him in his death, if somehow I may attain the resurrection from the dead" (Philippians 3:10–11).

Paul's undisputed letters and the Deuteropaulines indicate that he was a controversial figure from the start. We can see how controversial he was in the comment made in 2 Peter 3:16: "There are some things in them [Paul's letters] hard to understand, which the ignorant and unstable twist to their own destruction, as they do with other scriptures." Various groups within early Christianity, especially the Gnostics, used the figure of Paul to represent their own (sometimes heretical) positions. The great theologians in the Christian tradition (Origen, Augustine, Thomas Aquinas, Luther, Karl Barth) and the best modern biblical commentators have expended much time and ingenuity on trying to clarify Paul's theological thought. Thus they confirm that Paul's problems are our problems and that Paul's answers (correctly understood) can and should be our answers, too.

Bibliography

Barrett, C. K. *Paul: An Introduction to His Thought.* Louisville: Westminster John Knox, 1994.

Becker, Jürgen. *Paul: Apostle to the Gentiles.* Louisville: Westminster John Knox, 1994.

Dunn, James D. G. *The Theology of Paul the Apostle.* Grand Rapids: Eerdmans, 1998.

Fitzmyer, Joseph A. *Paul and His Theology.* Englewood Cliffs, NJ: Prentice-Hall, 1989.

Gaventa, Beverly Roberts. *Our Mother Saint Paul.* Louisville: Westminster John Knox, 2007.

Hengel, Martin. *The Pre-Christian Paul.* London: SCM, 1990.

Meeks, Wayne A. *The First Urban Christians: The Social World of the Apostle Paul.* New Haven: Yale University Press, 1983.

Murphy-O'Connor, Jerome. *Paul: A Critical Life.* Oxford: Clarendon Press, 1996.

———. *Paul the Letter Writer.* Collegeville: Liturgical Press, 1995.

———. *Paul: His Story.* Oxford—New York: Oxford University Press, 2004.

Sanders, E. P. *Paul: A Very Short Introduction.* Oxford—New York: Oxford University Press, 2001.

Schnelle, Udo. *The Apostle Paul: His Life and Theology*. Grand Rapids: Baker Academic, 2005.

Witherup, Ronald D. *101 Questions and Answers on Paul*. New York: Paulist Press, 2003.

———. *Saint Paul: Called to Conversion. A Seven-Day Retreat*. Cincinnati: St. Anthony Messenger, 2007.

Wright, N. T. *What Saint Paul Really Said*. Grand Rapids: Eerdmans, 1997.

———. *Paul in Fresh Perspective*. Minneapolis: Fortress, 2006.

For full commentaries on the New Testament writings pertaining to Paul, consult the pertinent volumes in the *Sacra Pagina* series edited by me and published by Liturgical Press, Collegeville, Minnesota. These volumes are now being reprinted in paperback editions with updated bibliographical supplements.

Byrne, Brendan. *Romans*. 1996.

Collins, Raymond F. *First Corinthians*. 1999.

Fiore, Benjamin. *Pastoral Epistles*. 2007.

Johnson, Luke T. *The Acts of the Apostles*. 1992.

Lambrecht, Jan. *Second Corinthians*. 1999.

MacDonald, Margaret. *Ephesians and Colossians*. 2000.

Matera, Frank J. *Galatians*. 1992.

Richard, Earl. *First and Second Thessalonians*. 1995.

Thurston, Bonnie B. and Judith M. Ryan. *Philippians and Philemon*. 2005.